Japanese
WORKBOOK

Lynne Strugnell

Japanese Workbook written by Lynne Strugnell

© 1995 Berlitz Publishing Co., Ltd.

Berlitz Publishing Co., Ltd., Berlitz House, Peterley Road, Oxford OX4 2TX, UK

Berlitz Publishing Co., Inc., 257 Park Avenue South, New York, NY 10010, USA

ISBN 2-8315-5083-1

First Printing 1995. Printed in UK.

CONTENTS

Introduction

For over a century, Berlitz language courses and books have helped people learn foreign languages for business, for pleasure and for travel – concentrating on the application of modern, idiomatic language in practical communication.

This *Berlitz Japanese Workbook* is designed for students who have learned enough Japanese for simple day-to-day communication and now want to improve their linguistic knowledge and confidence.

Maybe you are following an evening class or a self-study course and want some extra practice – or perhaps you learned Japanese some time ago and need to refresh your language skills. Either way, you will find the *Berlitz Japanese Workbook* an enjoyable and painless way to improve your Japanese.

How to Use the Workbook

We recommend that you set yourself a consistent weekly, or, if possible, daily study goal – one that you can achieve. The units gradually increase in difficulty and have a continuous storyline, so you will probably want to start at Unit 1.

Each unit focuses on a specific topic or situation: introducing yourself; going out for the evening; making purchases; travel and many more. Within the unit you will find exercises and word puzzles that build your vocabulary, grammar and communication skills. The exercises vary, but each unit follows the same basic sequence:

Match Game	relatively easy matching exercises that introduce each topic
Talking Point	a variety of exercises based on lively, idiomatic dialogues. Read these dialogues thoroughly, as they introduce the language you will use in the subsequent exercises
Word Power	imaginative vocabulary-building activities and games
Language Focus	specific practice in problem areas of grammar
Reading Corner	reading exercises in *hiragana*, *katakana* and *kanji*

We have provided space for you to write the answers into your Workbook if you wish, although you may prefer to write them on a separate sheet of paper.

If you want to check the meaning of a Japanese word, the Glossary at the back of the Workbook gives you its English translation. The Grammar section offers a handy overview of the essential structures covered in this Workbook, and you can check all of your answers against the Answer Key.

We wish you every success with your studies and hope that you will find the *Berlitz Japanese Workbook* not only helpful, but fun as well.

UNIT 1: Getting started

In this unit, you'll practice giving names and telephone numbers. You'll also practice nationalities, and saying who things belong to.

Match Game

1. Question and answers

Match each question to an appropriate response.

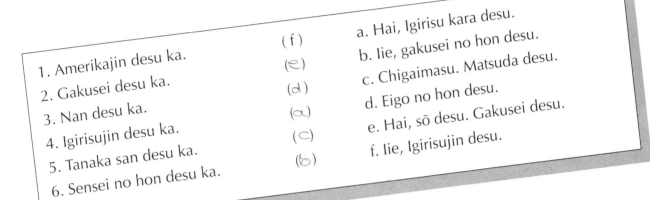

1. Amerikajin desu ka. (f)
2. Gakusei desu ka. (e)
3. Nan desu ka. (d)
4. Igirisujin desu ka. (a)
5. Tanaka san desu ka. (c)
6. Sensei no hon desu ka. (b)

a. Hai, Igirisu kara desu.
b. Iie, gakusei no hon desu.
c. Chigaimasu. Matsuda desu.
d. Eigo no hon desu.
e. Hai, sō desu. Gakusei desu.
f. Iie, Igirisujin desu.

Talking Point

2. Introductions

Kenji Matsuda, a student, is having coffee in the university before classes begin. He tries to start up a conversation with a foreigner sitting nearby, although she's rather reluctant to talk to him. Choose which words are appropriate to complete their conversation.

Kenji   Shitsurei desu ga, gakusei san desu ka.

Susan   (Hai/Iie), __Hai__ sō desu.

Kenji   Sō desu ka. Dochira kara desu ka. Amerikajin desu ka.

Susan   Iie, chigaimasu. Kanada (wa/kara) __kara__ desu.

Kenji   Aa, Kanadajin desu ka. Ii desu ne. *(handing her his name card)* Watashi (wa/no) __no__ meishi desu. Dōzo.

Susan   Arigatō.

Kenji	Matsuda desu. Matsuda Kenji. Hajimemashite.
Susan	Hajimemashite. (Watashi/Meishi) _Watashi_ wa Kūpā [Cooper] desu. Sūzan Kūpā.
Kenji	Kūpā san. Ii (gakusei/namae) _namae_ desu ne! *(pointing to his card)* Watashi no denwa bangō desu. (Sumimasen/Chigaimasu) _Sumimasen_ ga, Kūpā san no denwa bangō wa?
Susan	*(looking at her watch and standing up quickly)* Shitsurei shimasu. Kurasu no jikan desu.
Kenji	Demo...

Word Power

3. Telephone numbers

Write the telephone numbers in Kenji's phone book.

> **Example:** Matsuda san no denwa bangō wa zero-san no yon-san-yon-go no hachi-zero-hachi-ichi desu.

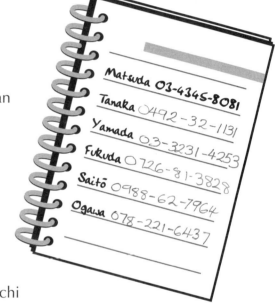

Matsuda 03-4345-8081
Tanaka 0492-32-1131
Yamada 03-3231-4253
Fukuda 0726-81-3828
Saitō 0988-62-7964
Ogawa 078-221-6437

1. Tanaka san no denwa bangō wa zero-yon-kyū-ni no san-ni no ichi-ichi-san-ichi desu.

2. Yamada san no denwa bangō wa zero-san no san-ni-san-ichi no yon-ni-go-san desu.

3. Fukuda san no denwa bangō wa zero-nana-ni-roku no hachi-ichi no san-hachi-ni-hachi desu.

4. Saitō sensei no denwa bangō wa zero-kyū-hachi-hachi no roku-ni no nana-kyū-roku-yon desu.

5. Ogawa san no denwa bangō wa zero-nana-hachi no ni-ni-ichi no roku-yon-san-nana desu.

Language Focus

4. Word order

Rearrange the words to make sentences.

1. ka/gakusei/san/wa/desu/Matsuda _Matsuda san wa gakusei desu ka_

2. meishi/no/desu/sensei _sensei no meishi desu_

3. kara/wa/san/Tōkyō/Tanaka/desu _Tanaka san wa Tōkyō kara desu_

4. 4163-7709/bangō/desu/denwa/wa   _denwa bangō wa 4163 7709 desu_

5. nan/ka/desu/namae/wa   _namae wa nan desu ka_

6. Furansujin/desu/wa/sensei/ka   _sensei wa Furansujin desu ka_

5. Where is it from?

Write a sentence about each country's products, as in the example.

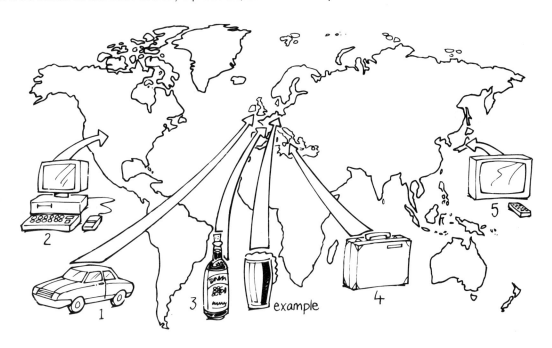

Example: _Doitsu no biiru desu._

1. _Igirisu no kuruma desu_
2. _Amerika no konpyūtā desu_
3. _Furansu no wain desu_
4. _Itaria no sūtsukēsu desu_
5. _Nihon no terebi desu_

6. Is it or isn't it?

Write questions and answers using the pictures, as in the example.

Example:

Q: (student?) _Gakusei desu ka._

A: _Iie, chigaimasu. Sensei desu._

1. (Mr Maeda's name card)

Q: _Maeda san no meishi desu ka?_ A: _Iie, chigaimasu. Matsuda san no desu._

2. (English book?)

Q: _Eigo no hon desu ka?_ A: _Hai, so desu._

3. (English car?)

Q: _Igirisu no kuruma desu ka?_ A: _Hai, so desu._

4. (Canadian?)

Q: _Kanada no furagu desu ka?_ A: _Iie, chigaimasu. Amerika no desu._

5. (Ms Ogawa's telephone number?)

Q: _Ogawa san no denwa bango desu ka._ A: _Hai, so desu._

 # Reading Corner

7. Match these *hiragana* characters to their sounds.

1. い _i_   2. あ _a_   3. う _u_

4. お _o_   5. え _e_

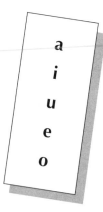

a
i
u
e
o

8. Read these words, and write them in *rōmaji* (roman letters).

1. うえ _ue_   2. いいえ _iie_   3. あい _ai_

4. あおい _aoi_   5. いえ _ie_

UNIT 2: Look at the time!

In this unit, you'll practice telling time, asking for personal information, and saying what something *isn't*.

Match Game

1. Look at the time!

Match the clocks to the times.

1. Jū-ichi-ji desu.
2. Ku-ji han desu.
3. San-ji han desu.
4. Shichi-ji desu.
5. Roku-ji han desu.

a. *shichi-ji desu*   b. *San-ji han desu*

c. *Jū-ichi-ji desu*

d. *Roku-ji han desu*   e. *Ku-ji han desu*

Talking Point

2. Wake up! You're late!

Kenji is dreaming in bed one morning, when he is awakened by the telephone ringing. It is Ms Hayashi, manager of the coffee shop where Kenji is supposed to be starting his part-time job today. Put the lines in order to find out what she says.

6 1. **Hayashi** Iie, osoi desu. Kissaten wa hachi-ji kara desu yo.

5 2. **Hayashi** Sō desu. Atarashii arubaito wa kyō kara desu. Demo Matsuda san wa mō osoi desu ne.

2 3. **Hayashi** Matsuda san, Hayashi desu.

4 4. **Hayashi** Hai, sō desu. Kissaten no Hayashi desu. Matsuda san, ima hachi-ji han desu yo.

7 5. **Kenji** *(suddenly awake)* Kissaten?! Aa! Arubaito! Atarashii arubaito! Kissaten no arubaito wa kyō kara desu!

3 6. **Kenji** *(puzzled)* Hayashi san desu ka.

9 7. **Kenji**   Hayashi san, sumimasen!

5 8. **Kenji**   Hachi-ji han desu ka. Hayai desu ne.

\ 9. **Kenji**   *(sleepily)* Moshi moshi, Matsuda desu.

Word Power

3. Categories

Assign the words below to the appropriate boxes.

konpyūtā, biiru, Nihongo, bideo, sensei, Eigo, wain, Amerikajin, Furansugo, gakusei, terebi, o-cha, Supeingo, rajio, kōhii, tomodachi

DRINKS	LANGUAGES	PEOPLE	ELECTRICAL GOODS
biiru	nihongo	sensei	konpyūtā
wain	eigo	amerikajin	bideo
o-cha	furansugo	gakusei	terebi
kōhii	supeingo	tomodachi	rajio

4. What's the time?

Draw the correct time on the clocks.

1. Jū-ni-ji han desu.

2. Ichi-ji han desu.

3. Hachi-ji desu.

4. Jū-ji han desu.

5. Ni-ji desu.

6. Yo-ji han desu.

Language Focus

5. Asking questions

Kenji's friend has been asking him about his new part-time job in the coffee shop. Look at Kenji's answers, and write down what his friend's questions were.

1. Arubaito wa ku-ji kara desu.

   Arubaito wa nan-ji kara desu ka.

2. Roku-ji made desu.

   Nan-ji made desu ka

3. Kissaten no namae wa "Dandelion" desu.

   Kissaten no namae wa nan desu ka

4. 03-4123-9931 desu.

   Denwa bangō wa nan desu ka

6. No, it isn't.

Look at the pictures, and write sentences like the one in the example.

Example: **Matsuda san ja arimasen.**

Tanaka san desu.

Matsuda   Tanaka

1. French Spanish

2. America   Canada

3. Coffee Tea

4. German   Italian

1. _Furansujin ja arimasen_
   Supeinjin desu.

2. _Amerika kara ja arimasen_
   Kanada kara desu.

3. _Kōhii ja arimasen_
   Kōcha desu.

4. _Doitsu no kuruma ja arimasen_
   Itaria no kuruma desu.

5. _Matsuda san no hon ja arimasen._
   Ogawa san no hon desu.

Mr Matsuda
Mr Ogawa

5.

7. All about you

Answer these questions about yourself.

1. O-namae wa nan desu ka.   Watashi no namae wa
   ∧ Nicola desu

2. Igirisujin desu ka.   Hai, igirisujin desu

3. Dochira kara desu ka.   Igirisu kara desu.

4. Gakusei san desu ka.   Hai, gakusei desu

Reading Corner

8. Choose the appropriate *rōmaji* equivalent from the box for each of the *hiragana* characters given below.

ka	ki	ke	ko	ku	ga	gi	gu	ge	go

1. ぎ _gi_   2. か _ka_   3. ぐ _gu_   4. け _ke_   5. こ _ko_

6. げ _ge_   7. く _ku_   8. が _ga_   9. き _ki_   10. ご _go_

9. Circle the word which has the pronunciation given at the beginning of the line.

1. akai (red)   a.おかい   **b.あかい**   c.おこい   d.あかえ

2. kaigi (meeting) a.かいき   b.かえぎ   c.かいぎい   **d.かいぎ**

3. koi (carp)   a.こえ   b.ごい   **c.こい**   d.かえ

4. eiga (movie)   a.いいが   b.えいか   c.いえが   **d.えいが**

5. keikaku (plan)   **a.けいかく**   b.けえかく   c.かいかく   d.けいがく

6. koe (voice)   a.こい   **b.こえ**   c.かい   d.ごえ

UNIT 3: Where is it?

In Unit 3, you'll practice describing where people and things are, talking about floors in department stores, and listing the things that are sold on each one.

Match Game

1. Complete the sentences.

Match the two parts of each sentence.

1. Matsuda san wa doko	(c)	a. wa nikai ni arimasu.
2. Watashi no heya	(a)	b. kissaten ni imasu.
3. Kenji san no tomodachi mo	(b)	c. ni imasu ka.
4. Kagi wa	(e)	d. ni arimasu.
5. Eigo no sensei	(f)	e. doko ni arimasu ka.
6. Watashi no kuruma wa asoko	(d)	f. wa soko ni imasu.

Talking Point

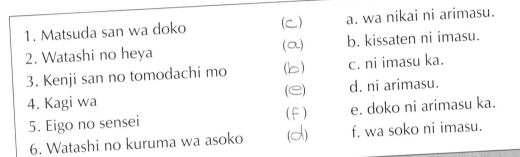

2. ni, no or wa?

Kenji just made it on time to the coffee shop where he's starting his part-time job today. The manager, Ms Hayashi, shows him where his locker is. Fill in the blanks with *ni, no,* or *wa* to complete their conversation (there are three of each).

Hayashi   Rokkā _wa_ kono heya _ni_ arimasu. Matsuda san _no_ rokkā wa koko desu. Dōzo.

Kenji   Dōmo arigatō. *(trying the door of the locker)* Sumimasen, kono doa wa chotto ...

Hayashi   Hmm, sō desu ne. Kagi _wa_ arimasen ne. Kono rokkā _no_ kagi wa doko ni arimasu ka. Saitō san? Saitō san!

Saitō   Hai, nan desu ka.

Hayashi   Kono rokkā _no_ kagi wa doko _ni_ arimasu ka.

Saitō   Nan-ban desu ka.

Hayashi   331-ban (san-san-ichi-ban) desu.

Saitō   Sumimasen. Kagi _wa_ koko _ni_ arimasu ga ....

Hayashi	Arigatō. *(taking the key and opening the locker door)* Hai, dōzo ... Ee?! Nani?
Kenji	*(laughing)* Neko! Neko ga imasu! Watashi no rokkā ni!
Hayashi	*(angry)* Dare no neko desu ka. Saitō san? Saitō san!
Saitō	Sumimasen. Watashi no neko desu ...

Word Power

3. Which department?

Can you find 10 items of clothing
in the word square?

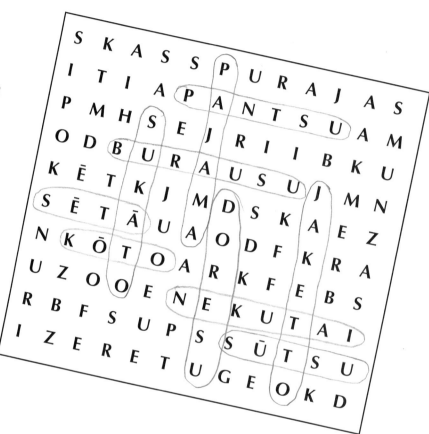

4. Connections

Look at the six groups of words below, and assign the rest of the
words from the box to the appropriate group.

dono	jūsu	go
	kyū	dōzo
rajio		shatsu
dōmo	arigatō	
eiga		pantsu
kono		kōcha
	yon	bideo
kutsu		biiru

1. ni, san — *go kyū yon*

2. sono, ano — *dono kono*

3. terebi, sutereo — *rajio eiga bideo*

4. o-cha, wain — *jūsu kōcha biiru*

5. sūtsu, burausu — *shatsu pantsu kutsu*

6. sumimasen, shitsurei shimasu — *dōzo dōmo arigato*

Language Focus

5. Which floor is it on?

Write the floor number on each floor of the department store. (Note that Japan uses the US system of floor numbering.)

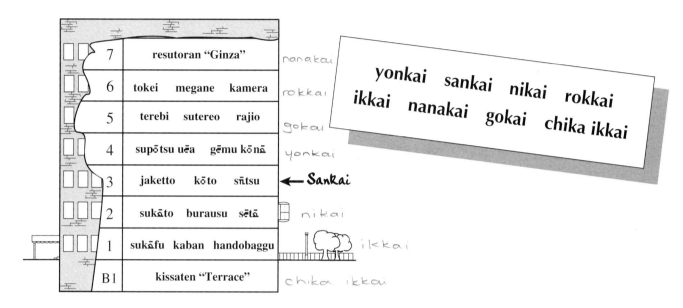

Some customers are at the information desk in the department store asking where certain goods are sold. Write questions and answers like the ones in the example, using the floor guide.

Example: (TVs and radios)

Q: Terebi to rajio wa nankai ni arimasu ka.

A: Gokai ni arimasu.

1. (coffee shop)

Q: Kissaten wa nankai ni arimasu ka

A: Chika ikkai ni arimasu

2. (briefcases and handbags)

Q: Kaban to handobaggu wa nankai ni arimasu ka

A: Ikkai ni arimasu

3. (skirts)

Q: Sukāto wa nankai ni arimasu ka

A: Nikai ni arimasu

4. (watches and cameras)

Q: Tokei to kamera wa nankai ni arimasu ka

A: Rokkai ni arimasu

5. (restaurant)

Q: Resutoran wa nankai ni arimasu ka

A: Nanakai ni arimasu

6. All about Kenji

Read the information about Kenji, and then put a check (✔) against the items which are connected to him, and a cross (✗) against the things which aren't.

Matsuda Kenji san no uchi wa ōkii desu. Apāto ja arimasen. Kenji san no heya wa nikai ni arimasu. Niwa ni, ōtobai ga arimasu. Kenji san wa kuruma wa arimasen ga, ōtobai wa arimasu. Ōkii ōtobai ja arimasen. Petto mo imasu. Kono petto no namae wa Kitty-chan desu ga, neko ja arimasen. Inu desu. Petto mo tomodachi mo imasu ga, gārufurendo wa imasen.

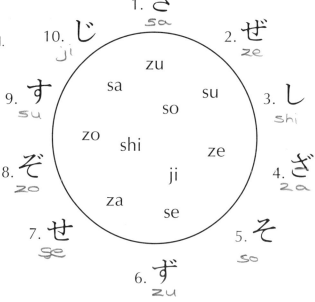

Reading Corner

7. Match each *hiragana* to the appropriate sound.

10. じ
ji

1. さ
sa

2. ぜ
ze

3. し
shi

4. ざ
za

5. そ
so

6. ず
zu

7. せ
se

8. ぞ
zo

9. す
su

(circle contents) zu, sa, su, so, zo, shi, ze, ji, za, se

8. Read the following words in *hiragana,* and pick out the ones which mean "over there" and "student." Then write all the words out in *rōmaji.*

1. いす
isu

2. かさ
kasa

3. ちいさい
chisai

4. がくせい — student
gakusei

5. あそこ
asoko
over there

6. しずか
shizuka

7. えき
eki

8. おおきい
ōkii

UNIT 4: Could I have a coffee, please?

In this unit, you'll again practice saying where things are, and telling time. You'll also practice asking for things.

Match Game

1. Where's the cat?

Match the cat to the location.

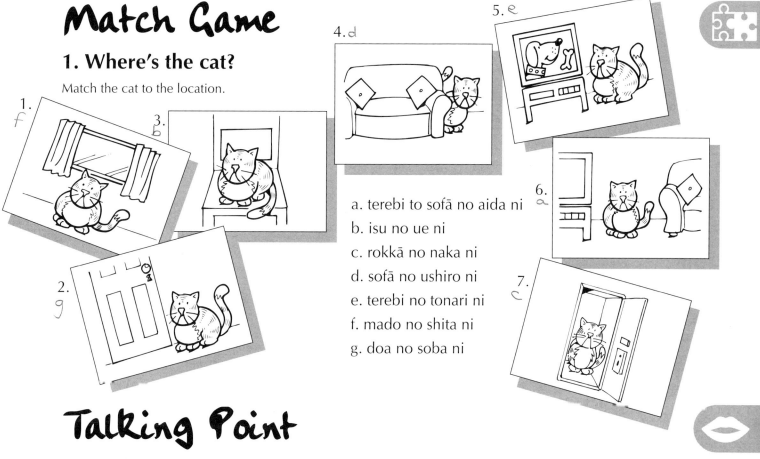

a. terebi to sofā no aida ni

b. isu no ue ni

c. rokkā no naka ni

d. sofā no ushiro ni

e. terebi no tonari ni

f. mado no shita ni

g. doa no soba ni

Talking Point

2. Serving a customer

After the cat in the locker fiasco, Ms Hayashi regains her composure, and quickly shows Kenji where things are in the coffee shop. Choose the appropriate words from the box to complete their conversation. (Be careful – there are two words too many.)

o-genki	sumimasen	shitsurei	koko	arimasen
kudasai	kono	konban	daigaku	doko

Hayashi Naifu to fōku to supūn wa _kono_ hikidashi no naka ni arimasu. Napukin wa _koko_ desu. Ii desu ka.

Kenji Hai, wakarimashita.

Hayashi	*(A customer comes in.)* Matsuda san, o-kyakusan desu yo. *(loudly)* Irasshaimase!
Customer	Hotto o _kudasai_ .
Kenji	Hai, ... *(recognizing her)* Aa! Kūpā san desu ne.
Customer	Hai, sō desu. _Shitsurei_ desu ga...
Kenji	Matsuda desu. Matsuda Kenji. Onaji _daigaku_ no gakusei desu.
Customer	*(unenthusiastic)* Aa, sō desu ne, Matsuda san desu ne ...
Kenji	Kūpā san wa _o genki_ desu ka.
Customer	Hai, o-kage sama de. Sumimasen ga, watashi no kōhii ...
Kenji	Kūpā san, _konban_ totemo ii konsāto ga arimasu ga ...
Customer	Sumimasen. Jikan ga _arimasen_. Kōhii o kudasai!
Kenji	Demo ...
Hayashi	Matsuda san! Mondai desu ka.
Kenji	*(flustered)* Iie, shitsurei shimashita.

Word Power

3. What's the time?

Draw the correct time on the clocks.

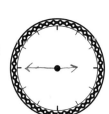

1. go-ji go-Jip-pun

2. jū-ji jū-go-fun

3. ichi-ji ni-jip-pun

4. san-ji yon-jū-go-fun

5. hachi-ji go-fun

Language Focus

4. When's the concert?

Write sentences giving the starting and finishing times of the situations shown below.

Example: Konsāto wa hachi-ji han kara ku-ji yon-jū-go-fun made desu.

Concert Tonight!

8.30 - 9.45

1. Eiga wa ni-ji-jippun kara san-ji-go-jippun made desu
2. Resutoran wa roku-ji han kara jū-ichi-ji-yon-jū-go-fun made desu
3. Kissaten wa hachi-ji kara roku-ji-han made desu.
4. Eigo no kurasu wa san-ji-jū-go-fun kara go-ji-jū-go-fun made desu
5. Depāto wa jū-ji kara roku-ji-han made desu

5. Kenji's room

Look at the picture of Kenji's room, and draw in the items described below.

Kenji san no heya wa totemo kitanai desu. Beddo no shita ni, hon to zasshi ga arimasu. Beddo to tsukue no aida ni, ōtobai no taiya ga arimasu. Taiya no tonari ni, tenisu raketto to bōru ga arimasu. Tsukue no ue ni, kasetto tēpu to CD [shii dii] ga takusan arimasu. Doa no ushiro ni, kōto to pajama ga arimasu. Kenji san wa ima imasen ga, Kitty-chan (Kenji san no inu) wa beddo no ue ni imasu.

6. Find the mistake.

One of the sentences in each pair contains a mistake. Put a check (✓) against the correct sentence, and a cross (✗) against the one with the mistake.

1. __✓__   a. Sono kissaten wa atarashii desu.

    __✗__   b. Sono wa atarashii kissaten desu.

2. ＼‿ a. Kuruma no kagi wa doko ni arimasu ka.

   ✗ b. Kuruma kagi wa doko ni arimasu ka.

3. ✗ a. Matsuda wa uchi ni imasen.

   ＼‿ b. Matsuda san wa uchi ni imasen.

4. ✗ a. Nihongo no kurasu wa nan-ji kara made desu ka.

   ＼‿ b. Nihongo no kurasu wa nan-ji kara nan-ji made desu ka.

5. ＼‿ a. Saitō san no neko wa rokkā no naka ni imasu.

   ✗ b. Saitō san no rokkā wa, neko no naka ni imasu.

Reading Corner

7. Choose the appropriate *rōmaji* equivalent for each of the *hiragana* characters below.

to	ji	de	ta	tsu
da	chi	do	te	zu

1. で _de_ 2. ち _chi_ 3. と _to_ 4. づ _zu_ 5. た _ta_

6. つ _tsu_ 7. て _te_ 8. だ _da_ 9. ぢ _ji_ 10. ど _do_

8. Match the English and Japanese *rōmaji* words, and then circle the same words in *hiragana*.

1. university   2. where?   3. please give me ...   4. job, work   5. chair   6. student
d   f   h   k   b   i

7. watch   8. is, are   9. please, go ahead   10. shoes   11. movie   12. desk
j   a   e   i   c   g

a. desu b. isu c. eiga d. daigaku e. dōzo f. doko
g. tsukue h. kudasai i. kutsu j. tokei k. shigoto l. gakusei

あしごとけいさえだいがくつくえたえいがくせい
くださいすぞどこがどうぞあいですおち

UNIT 5: Like it or hate it?

In Unit 5 you'll practice talking about everyday activities, and likes and dislikes.

Match Game

1. Verbs

Match each picture to an appropriate verb.

a. yomimasu

b. kakimasu

c. kikimasu

d. nomimasu

e. tsukurimasu

f. mimasu

g. kaerimasu

h. denwa shimasu

Talking Point

2. Kenji's birthday

Today is Kenji's birthday, and tonight the family are going out to dinner to celebrate. Mrs Matsuda is just on her way home from work, and is telling a colleague about the evening's plans. Fill in an appropriate verb to complete their conversation.

tsukurimasen desu (x3) kaerimasu shimasu ikimasu
tsukurimasu nomimasen ikimasu wakarimasen arimasen

Mrs Wada   Matsuda san, kōhii o __nomimasen__ ka.

Mrs Matsuda   Sumimasen ga, kyō wa jikan ga __arimasen__. Sugu uchi e __kaerimasu__. Kyō wa Kenji no tanjōbi __desu__.

Mrs Wada   Aa, Kenji san no tanjōbi desu ka. Ii __desu__ ne. Kēki o __tsukurima__ ka.

Mrs Matsuda	Iie, _tsukurimasen_. Ryōri ga dai-kirai desu.
Mrs Wada	Sō desu ka. Ja, nani o _shimasu_ ka.
Mrs Matsuda	Minna issho ni resutoran e _ikimasu_.
Mrs Wada	Doko no resutoran?
Mrs Matsuda	Mada _wakarimasen_ Kenji wa Indo ryōri ga dai-suki desu ga, watashitachi wa kirai _desu_. Watashi wa Nihon ryōri ga suki desu ga, Tomoko wa hanbāgā dake suki desu.
Mrs Wada	Aa, Tomoko chan mo issho ni resutoran e _ikimasu_ ka.
Mrs Matsuda	*(sighing)* Hai. Sore wa mondai desu. Kenji to Tomoko wa itsumo kenka shimasu. Resutoran no naka de mo itsumo kenka shimasu.

Word Power

3. Daily activities

Number the activities 1–8 to show the order in which you usually do them, and then draw the time you do them on the clock.

__3__ shinbun o yomimasu

__7__ bangohan o tsukurimasu

__1__ okimasu

__4__ kaisha/gakkō e ikimasu

__2__ asagohan o tabemasu

__8__ nemasu

__6__ terebi o mimasu

__5__ hirugohan o tabemasu

Language Focus

4. Word order

Ask questions 1-6 correctly to find out more information about Kenji's mother.

1. itsumo/wa/ni/Matsuda/okimasu/nan-ji/san/ka _Matsuda san wa itsumo nan-ji ni okimasu ka_
   6:30 ni.

2. shigoto/kanojo/shimasu/donna/wa/o/ka _Kanojo wa donna shigoto o shimasu ka._
   Fasshon dezainā desu.

3. ga/wa/shigoto/suki/Matsuda/sono/desu/san/ka _Matsuda san wa sono shigoto ga suki desu ka_
   Hai, dai-suki desu.

4. no/doko/ikimasu/konban/e/resutoran/ka _konban____doko no resutoran e ikimasu ka_

Mada wakarimasen.

5. asagohan/dare/tsukurimasu/o/itsumo/ga/ka _dare ga asagohan o tsukurimasu ka._ (itsumo)

Matsuda san desu.

5. Love or hate?

Rearrange these phrases in order of strongest like to strongest dislike, adding words of your own to complete the sentences.

a. __ ga mā-mā suki desu   d. __ ga dai-suki desu

b. __ ga kirai desu   e. __ ga suki desu

c. __ ga dai-kirai desu   f. __ ga amari suki ja arimasen.

LOVE 1. _____ga dai-suki desu_____

2. _____ga suki desu_____

3. _____ga māmā suki desu_____

4. _____ga amari suki ja arimasen_____

5. _____ga kirai desu_____

HATE 6. _____ga dai-kirai desu_____

6. Do you like to go bowling?

Mrs Matsuda, Kenji, and Tomoko, his younger sister, considered various possibilities before deciding to go to a restaurant to celebrate Kenji's birthday. Look at the chart, and write sentences like the ones in the example.

	Mrs Matsuda	Kenji	Tomoko
ice skating?	dislike	not much	love
movie?	like very much	like very much	so-so
bowling?	like	dislike	like
kabuki theatre?	like	dislike	hate

Example: Kenji san/kabuki?   Q: _Kenji san wa kabuki ga suki desu ka._

A: _Iie, kirai desu._

1. Matsuda san/bōringu?   Q: _Matsuda san wa bōringu ga suki desu ka_

A: _Hai, suki desu_

2. Kenji san/aisu sukēto?   Q: _Kenji san wa sukēto ga suki desu ka_ (aisu)

A: _Iie, amari suki ja arimasen_

3. Tomoko chan/kabuki?

Q: Tomoko san wa kabuki ga suki desuta.

A: Iie, dai-kirai desu.

4. Matsuda san/aisu sukēto

Q: Matsuda san wa aisu sukēto ga suki desu ka.

A: Iie, kirai desu.

5. Matsuda san to Kenji san/eiga?

Q: Matsuda san to Kenji san wa eiga ga kirai desu ka

A: Hai, dai-suki desu

Reading Corner

7. Circle the *hiragana* characters for *na, ni, nu, ne,* and *no*.

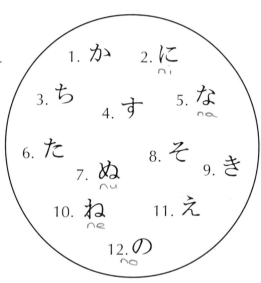

1. か　2. に (ni)
3. ち　4. す　5. な (na)
6. た　7. ぬ (nu)　8. そ　9. き
10. ね (ne)　11. え
12. の (no)

8. Find the words in *hiragana* which mean the same as the English words.

1. いぬ (inu) [g]	2. なか (naka) [b]	3. なに (nani) [f]	4. だいすき (daisuki) [e]	5. この (kono) [c]
6. おなじ (onaji) [a]	7. しごと (shigoto) [i]	8. その (sono) [h]	9. ねこ (neko) [d]	10. うち (uchi) [k]

a. same	b. inside	c. this	d. cat	e. like very much
f. what?	g. dog	h. that	i. work	k. home

UNIT 6: Do you come here often?

Unit 6 provides more practice talking about daily activities and how often you do them, and there is also some work on the family, and giving people's ages.

Match Game

1. Opposites

Join the words that are opposites.

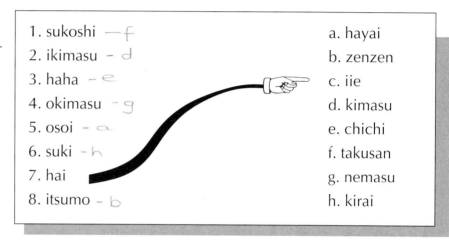

1. sukoshi —f	a. hayai
2. ikimasu - d	b. zenzen
3. haha - e	c. iie
4. okimasu - g	d. kimasu
5. osoi - a	e. chichi
6. suki - h	f. takusan
7. hai	g. nemasu
8. itsumo - b	h. kirai

Talking Point

2. At the restaurant

Mr and Mrs Matsuda, Kenji, and Tomoko are at the restaurant to celebrate Kenji's birthday. Kenji pours the beer for everyone, ready for a toast. Complete their conversation by writing Kenji's lines in the right place.

1. Otōsan wa?	2. Mada wakai yo. Biiru wa dame desu.
3. Uso! Uisukii wa kirai!	4. Dame desu yo, Tomoko. Mada 13-sai deshō?
5. Okāsan, biiru wa?	6. Tomoko wa? Jūsu?

Kenji   _Okāsan, biiru wa?_

Mrs Matsuda Hai, sukoshi onegai shimasu.

Kenji   _Otōsan wa?_

Mr Matsuda   Aa, dōmo.

Kenji	_Tomoko wa? Jūsu?_
Tomoko	Iie, watashi mo biiru.
Kenji	_Dame desu yo, Tomoko. Mada 13-sai deshō?_
Tomoko	Iie, 14-sai desu.
Kenji	_Mada wakai yo. Biiru wa dame desu._
Tomoko	_(loudly)_ Demo, o-niisan wa maiban uisukii mo biiru mo ...
Kenji	_(angrily)_ _Uso! Uisukii wa kirai!_
Mr Matsuda	Urusai! Mō ii desu. Kyō wa Kenji no tanjōbi deshō? Ja, Tomoko, biiru o sukoshi dake, dōzo.
Tomoko	Arigatō.
Mrs Matsuda	Hai, kanpai!
Everyone	Kanpai! Kenji, omedetō gozaimasu.

Word Power

3. My family, your family

Look at the words listed below, and write "M" by those which are male, and "F" by those which are female. Then put a check (✔) in the box at the side of each word for a member of your family and a cross (✘) for someone else's family.

_f_ okusan ✘	_f_ ane ✔	_f_ haha ✔	_m_ o-tōsan ✘
_f_ imōtosan ✘✔	_m_ chichi ✔	_m_ o-niisan ✘	_m_ otōto ✔
_f_ o-kāsan ✘	_m_ go-shujin ✘	_f_ kanai ✔	_m_ shujin ✔
_f_ o nēsan ✘	_m_ ani ✔	_f_ imōtō ✔	_m_ otōtosan ✘

4. The family tree

Look at Kenji's family tree, and write sentences about how old everyone is.

Example: (Kenji) **Kenji san wa ni-jū-is-sai desu.**

1. (mother) Kenji san no okāsan wa yon-jū-nana-sai desu.
2. (father) Kenji san no otōsan wa yon-jū-has-sai desu.
3. (younger sister) Kenji san no imōtosan wa jū-yon-sai desu
4. (older sister) Onēsan wa ni-jū-go-sai desu.
5. (sister's husband) O-nēsan no go-shujin wa ni-jū-roku-sai desu

Language Focus

5. Always, often, sometimes, seldom, never

Answer these questions about yourself, using one of the words in the box.

Example: Yoku uisukii o nomimasu ka.

Hai, yoku nomimasu./Tokidoki nomimasu./Iie, amari nomimasen.

1. Yoku Nihongo o hanashimasu ka. _Iie, amari hanashimasen_
2. Yoku eiga o mimasu ka. _Hai, yoku mimasu_
3. Tokidoki sushi o tabemasu ka. _Iie, zenzen tabemasen_
4. Opera o yoku kikimasu ka. _Iie, amari kikimasen_
5. Tokidoki depāto de kaimono o shimasu ka. _Hai, tokidoki shimasu_
6. Yoku kēki o tsukurimasu ka. _Hai, tokidoki tsukurimasu_
7. Itsumo terebi de nyūsu o mimasu ka. _Iie, tokidoki mimasu_
8. Yoku tegami o kakimasu ka. _Hai, yoku kakimasu_

> **itsumo**
> **yoku**
> **tokidoki**
> **amari**
> **zenzen**

6. Locations + *de*

Kenji's mother has her sister Sachiko coming to visit tomorrow. Look at the picture and write sentences about how they plan to spend the day.

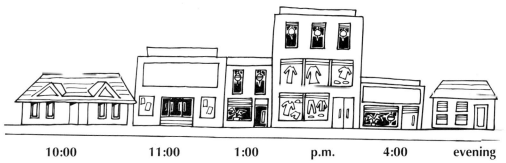

10:00   11:00   1:00   p.m.   4:00   evening

Example: *10:00 ni eki de Sachiko ni aimasu.*

1. 11:00 ni _Supōtsu sentā de tenisu o shimasu_
2. 1:00 ni _Resutoran de hirugohan o tabemasu_
3. Gogo ni _Depāto de kaimono o shimasu_
4. 4:00 ni _kissaten de kōhī o nomimasu_
5. Yoru ni _uchi de bangohan o tsukurimasu_

> **Train station** – meet Sachiko
> **Sports center** – tennis
> **Restaurant** – lunch
> **Department store** – shopping
> **Coffee shop** – coffee
> **Evening** – cook dinner

Reading Corner

7. Write the *rōmaji* equivalent next to each *hiragana* character.

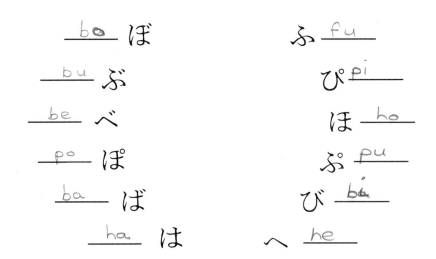

ba ぼ   ふ fu

bu ぶ   ぴ pi

be べ   ほ ho

po ぽ   ぷ pu

ba ば   び bi

ha は   へ he

8. Circle the word in *hiragana* which is the same as the one given at the beginning of the line.

1. ikebana (flower arranging)   a. いけはな   (b.) いけばな   c. いけはな

2. hanabi (fireworks)   a. へなび   b. はなべ   (c.) はなび

3. kabuki (traditional theater)   a. かぶけ   (b.) かぶき   c. かぷき

4. heta (unskillful)   (a.) へた   b. ひた   c. へな

5. hosoi (slim)   a. はそい   b. ぽそい   (c.) ほそい

6. fune (boat)   (a.) ふね   b. ふぬ   c. ぷね

UNIT 7: Is it expensive?

Unit 7 provides practice with large numbers, prices, colors, and describing things.

Match Game

1. -i adjectives

Match the words or phrases which have a similar meaning.

1. tsumaranai	(g)	a. samuku arimasen
2. ii	(d)	b. oishiku arimasen
3. atsui	(a)	c. takaku arimasen
4. kuroi	(i)	d. waruku arimasen
5. atarashii	(h)	e. muzukashiku arimasen
6. kantan	(e)	f. hayaku arimasen
7. mazui	(b)	g. omoshiroku arimasen
8. yasui	(c)	h. furuku arimasen
9. osoi	(f)	i. shiroku arimasen

Talking Point

2. At the coffee shop

Mrs Matsuda and her sister Sachiko have come to Kenji's coffee shop for a break during their afternoon's shopping, and they are trying to decide what to have. Read through their conversation, and then see if the statements which follow it are true or false.

Mrs Matsuda Kēki wa, nani ga oishii? Sono chokorēto no kēki wa?

Kenji Iie, *(whispering)* o-kāsan, sore wa amari ...

Mrs Matsuda Sō desu ka. Ja, remon pai wa?

Kenji Remon pai wa totemo amai yo.

Sachiko *(laughing)* Kenji, kono kissaten no kēki wa zenbu oishiku arimasen ka.

Kenji Chiizukēki wa oishii yo. Demo, chotto takai desu.

Sachiko Ikura desu ka.

Kenji Sen hyaku en.

Sachiko Sen hyaku en? Takai desu ne. Ja, kōhii dake de ii desu. *(whispering)* Kenji, kono kissaten wa amari yoku arimasen ne. Iro mo chotto ...

Mrs Matsuda Sō desu ne – pinku to murasaki ...

Kenji   Demo kōhii wa oishii desu yo. Sore kara, ongaku mo ii desu ne.

Mrs Matsuda Chotto urusai desu ga ...

1. Matsuda san wa chokorēto no kēki o tabemasu.   *True/False*
2. Remon pai wa amari amaku arimasen.   *True/False*
3. Kissaten no kēki wa zenbu oishiku arimasen.   *True/False*
4. Sachiko san wa chiizukēki o tabemasen.   *True/False*
5. Sachiko san wa, kissaten no iro ga suki ja arimasen.   *True/False*
6. Kenji san wa, kissaten no ongaku ga suki desu.   *True/False*

Word Power

3. Colors

The following 12 colors are hidden in the word square, horizontally, vertically, and diagonally. (There are two ways of saying "blue" and "green.") Can you find them?

red	white
black	blue x 2
yellow	green x 2
brown	pink
orange	purple

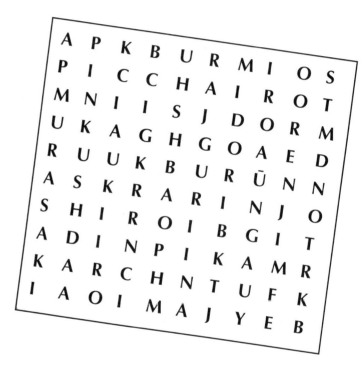

4. Large numbers

Find the appropriate number to go with the words.

1. ni-sen san-byaku
2. ni-man san-zen
3. san-man go-hyaku go-jū
4. san-byaku jū
5. has-sen hap-pyaku san-jū
6. sen san-byaku
7. jū-man go-sen
8. ichi-man go-sen rop-pyaku

2,300   105,000   470
30,550   8,830   310   1,560
                              23,000
15,600   1,400   15,000   301
1,300   230   80,830

Language Focus

5. How much?

Mrs Matsuda and Sachiko have had a successful day's shopping. Look at the items they bought, and write how much each one cost.

Example: (coat) *Kōto wa kyū-man go-sen en deshita.*

----

1. (handbag)

    ----

2. (sweater)

    ----

3. (scarf)

    ----

4. (watch)

    ----

5. (magazine)

    ----

6. (skirt)

¥940
¥21,000
¥7,500
¥95,000
¥14,300
¥6,400
¥22,900

6. Word order

Rearrange the groups of words to make questions. (Be careful – there is one word too many in each group.)

1. wa/desu/akai/no/kono/dare/imōto/sukāfu/ka

    Imōto no desu.

2. muzukashii/arubaito/kantan/desu/Kenji/wa/no/san/ka

    Iie, zenzen muzukashiku arimasen.

3. wa/ga/Matsuda/shimasu/suki/san/desu/kaimono/ka

    Hai, dai-suki desu.

4. urusai/ongaku/wa/kikimasu/desu/no/kissaten/ka

    Hai, chotto urusai desu.

5. ikura/kutsu/wa/atarashii/deshita/nani/Matsuda/no/san/ka

¥26,500 deshita.

6. desu/wa/oishii/ano/resutoran/o/atarashii/ka

Iie, amari oishiku arimasen.

Reading Corner

7. Match the words in *hiragana* to their *rōmaji* equivalents.

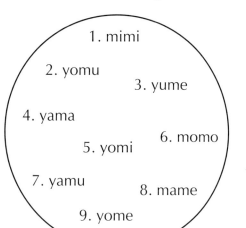

1. mimi
2. yomu
3. yume
4. yama
5. yomi
6. momo
7. yamu
8. mame
9. yome

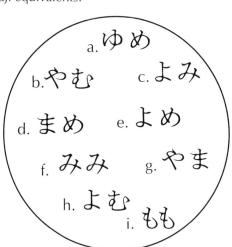

a. ゆめ
b. やむ
c. よみ
d. まめ
e. よめ
f. みみ
g. やま
h. よむ
i. もも

8. Find the Japanese equivalents of the words listed below in the puzzle. They are lined up horizontally, vertically, and diagonally.

1. How do you do?
2. shopping
3. cold
4. room
5. always
6. early
7. every day
8. read
9. often
10. name card
11. letter
12. sweet
13. glasses

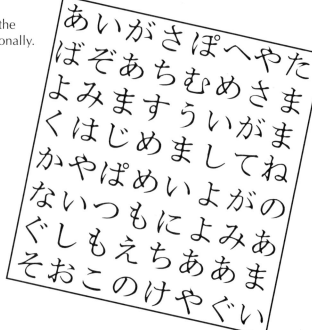

あいがさぽへやた
ばぞあちむめさま
よみますういがま
くはじめましてね
かやぱめいよがの
ないつもによみあ
ぐしもえちああま
そおこのけやぐい

UNIT 8: What did you do on the weekend?

In Unit 8 you'll practice describing things which happened in the past, days of the week, schedules, and forms of transportation.

Match Game

1. Verbs in the past

Match each word or phrase on the left with an appropriate verb on the right.

1. tomodachi ni
2. sērusu repōto o
3. Amerika e
4. atarashii sētā o
5. haha ni denwa
6. Furansugo no eiga ga
7. byōki ni
8. amari suki

( ) a. wakarimasen deshita
( ) b. narimashita
( ) c. shimashita
( ) d. aimashita
( ) e. ja arimasen deshita
( ) f. kakimashita
( ) g. ikimasen deshita
( ) h. kaimashita

Talking Point

2. The weekend

It's Monday morning, and on the train to work Mr Matsuda is talking to an acquaintance about the weekend. Use all the verbs below to fill in the blanks and complete their conversation. (Some of the verbs are in the negative.)

Ishii   Matsuda san, daijōbu desu ka. Amari genki ja arimasen ne.

Matsuda Sō, amari ii shūmatsu (-) _ja arimasen deshita._

Ishii   Dō (+) _ _ _ _ _ _ _ _ _ _ _ _ _ ka.

Matsuda Kinyōbi no yoru, byōki ni (+) _ _ _ _ _ _ _ _ _ _ _ _ _ _ _ _ .

Ishii   Byōki desu ka. Demo, kinyōbi no yoru, Indo ryōri no resutoran e (+) _ _ _ _ _ _ _ _ _ _ _ _ _ _ _ _ _ ne.

Matsuda Sō desu. Musuko no tanjōbi (+) _ _ _ _ _ _ _ _ _ _ _ _ _ _ _ _ .

narimashita x 2
kaerimashita deshita x 5
shimashita
kaimashita
ikimashita x 2
tabemashita
nomimashita x 2

33

Ishii Resutoran no ryōri wa dame (+) _____ ka.

Matsuda Wakarimasen ne. Kanai mo Kenji mo Tomoko mo takusan (+) _____ ga, daijōbu (+) _____.

Ishii Dō shite deshō. Takusan (+) _____ ka.

Matsuda Iie, amari (-) _____.

Ishii Sō desu ka. Ja, ii shūmatsu (-) _____ ne.

Matsuda Sō, zenzen dame deshita. Takai purezento o (+) _____. Takai resutoran e (+) _____. Sore kara, resutoran de byōki ni (+) _____ kara, takai takushii de (+) _____. O-kane wa mō arimasen.

Word Power

3. Days of the week

Write in the days of the week to complete the puzzle.

4. Transportation

Look at the picture and write sentences about how Mrs Matsuda's sister Sachiko made it to her home near Osaka with all her luggage and shopping.

Example: Magome eki made kuruma de ikimashita.

1. _____
2. _____
3. _____
4. _____
5. _____

Language Focus

5. What did he do?

Mr Matsuda has had a busy week, and has hardly seen anything of his family. Look at his schedule, and write questions and answers about what he's been doing.

Getsu	Ōsaka e
	Kaigi
	Guriin Hoteru
Ka	Kaigi
	Tōkyō e
Sui	Ōsaka shutchō no repōto
	Yokohama de kaigi
Moku	Haha no tanjōbi
	Haha ni denwa
Kin	
	Wada san to bangohan

Example: (Mon./a.m.)

Q: Getsuyōbi no asa, nani o shimashita ka.

A: Ōsaka e ikimashita.

1. **Q:** (Tue./p.m.)

   A:

2. **Q:** (Tue./evening)

   A:

3. **Q:** (Wed./a.m.)

   A:

4. **Q:** (Thu./a.m.)

   A:

5. **Q:** (Fri./evening)

   A:

6. Things to do

Mr Matsuda made a list of the things he had to do before he went on his business trip to Osaka, but he didn't manage to do all of them. Write sentences about what he did and didn't do.

✗ haha no tanjōbi no purezento (buy)
✗ 1. haha ni tegami (write)
✓ 2. Ōsaka Hoteru ni denwa (call)
✗ 3. Ōsaka shisha no sērusu repōto (read)
✓ 4. kuroi sūtsu (buy)
✗ 5. Ōsaka no o-kyakusan to (speak to)

Example: O-kāsan no tanjōbi no purezento o kaimasen deshita.

1.

2.

3.

4.

5.

7. Asking questions

You are talking to someone on the telephone, but it's a bad line, and you can't hear them very well. Ask questions to confirm the information you didn't hear clearly.

Example: ***** to issho ni Ōsaka e ikimashita.
Sumimasen, dare to issho ni ikimashita ka. _____

1. ***** kara takushii de kimashita. _____

2. Kinō no asa ***** ni okimashita. _____

3. Kinyōbi no yoru, ***** de bangohan o tabemashita. _____

4. Ano atarashii depāto de ***** o kaimashita. _____

5. Nyū Yōku de ***** o takusan mimashita. _____

6. Rondon de ***** ni aimashita yo. _____

Reading Corner

8. Match the *hiragana* characters to the appropriate *rōmaji* equivalents.

1. る	5. ん	a. ra	e. ro
2. を	6. わ	b. ri	f. wa
3. ろ	7. り	c. ru	g. wo
4. ら	8. れ	d. re	h. n

9. Write these kana words in *rōmaji,* and then match them to the English equivalents.

1. でんわをします _____
2. おもしろい _____
3. ひるごはん _____
4. わかりました _____
5. しつれいします _____

6. あたらしい _____
7. ありがとう _____
8. わるい _____
9. いくら _____
10. うしろ _____

a. interesting	b. new	c. thank you	d. behind	e. telephone
f. how much?	g. lunch	h. bad	i. I understand	j. excuse me

36

UNIT 9: The interview was difficult.

In this unit, there is more practice with the past tense, time phrases, and saying the year.

Match Game

1. Years

Match the words to the numbers.

1. sen kyū-hyaku kyū-jū-nana-nen
2. sen kyū-hyaku roku-jū-nen
3. sen kyū-hyaku hachi-jū-san-nen
4. sen nana-hyaku nana-jū-kyū-nen
5. sen hap-pyaku kyū-jū-san-nen
6. sen kyū-hyaku yon-jū-roku-nen
7. sen kyū-hyaku kyū-jū-ni-nen
8. sen kyū-hyaku nana-jū-kyū-nen

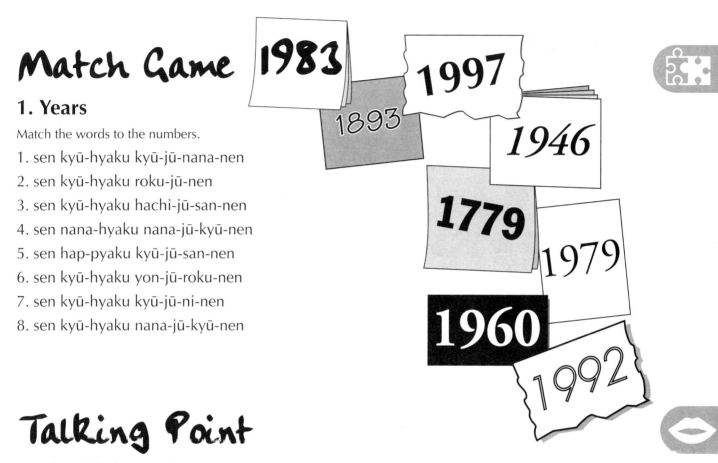

1983
1997
1893
1946
1779
1979
1960
1992

Talking Point

2. The job interview

Yesterday Kenji went for a job interview at an American company, and today one of his lecturers is asking him about it. Read through their conversation, and then see if the statements which follow it are true or false.

Sensei   Kinō no mensetsu wa dō deshita ka.

Kenji   Totemo muzukashikatta! Zenzen dame deshita.

Sensei   Sō? Dō shite desu ka. Shitsumon wa muzukashikatta desu ka.

Kenji   Iie, shitsumon wa sonna ni muzukashiku nakatta kedo, Amerika no kaisha deshō? Dakara minna Eigo de hanashimashita! Yo-nin imashita – Amerika-jin futari to Nihon-jin futari. Totemo hazukashikatta desu.

Sensei   Daijōbu deshō. Matsuda san wa Eigo ga jōzu desu yo.

Kenji   Iie, iie, sonna koto wa arimasen. Iroiro-na shitsumon ga arimashita. "Doko ni umaremashita ka. O-tōsan wa donna shigoto o shimasu ka. Kyōdai wa nan-nin imasu ka. Shumi wa nan desu ka." Taihen deshita!

Sensei	Sō desu ka. Kūpā san mo sō iimashita.
Kenji	Kūpā san? Sūzan Kūpā?
Sensei	Hai. Kūpā san mo ototoi onaji kaisha de mensetsu ga arimashita.
Kenji	Ee?!

1. Kūpā san no mensetsu mo, Kenji san no mensetsu mo kinō deshita.   *True/False*
2. Mensetsu wa, Amerika no kaisha de arimashita.   *True/False*
3. Kenji san wa, Eigo ga muzukashii to omoimasu.   *True/False*
4. Amerika no kaisha no hito wa futari imashita.   *True/False*
5. Amerika-jin mo Nihon-jin mo Eigo de shitsumon o shimashita.   *True/False*
6. Kūpā san mo sensei to mensetsu no hanashi o shimashita.   *True/False*

Word Power

3. Odd man out

Which word doesn't fit in each of the groups below?

1. natsu   atsui   fuyu   aki   haru
2. yoru   asa   gogo   konbanwa   ban
3. ashita   kinō   kyonen   ototoi   otōto
4. san-nin   hidari   jū-nin   futari   hitori
5. tanoshikatta   samukatta   atsukatta   atatakakatta   suzushikatta
6. hanashimashita   iimashita   denwa shimashita   shitsumon shimashita   kaerimashita

4. Time phrases

Rearrange the following words or phrases in order, beginning with the most recent.

1. senshū no kinyōbi   _____
2. kinō no ban   _____
3. kyonen no aki   _____
4. go-nen mae   _____
5. ima   _____
6. ototoi   _____
7. ototoshi   _____
8. san-nen mae   _____
9. kesa   _____

Language Focus

5. About Susan

Here are some of the notes taken by one of the Americans at Susan Cooper's job interview. Write sentences about Susan, using the notes.

Example: <u>Sen kyū-hyaku nana-jū-nen ni Toronto ni</u>
<u>umaremashita.</u> born in Toronto (1970)

1. _____

2. _____

3. _____

4. _____

5. _____

> 1. '82 - '85 lived in England (with family)
> 2. studied economics at university
> 3. also Spanish
> 4. '92 - '93 taught English in Spain
> 5. came to Japan (1993)

6. When I was a child ...

Write sentences comparing how things were when you were a child, and how they are now, as in the example.

Example: (swimming/good at – not very good at)

<u>Kodomo no toki, suiei ga jōzu deshita ga, ima wa amari jōzu</u>
<u>ja arimasen.</u>

1. _____

2. _____

3. _____

4. _____

5. _____

6. _____

eyesight was poor	okay
lived in London	live in Paris
didn't like cheese	love it
often played sport	never play sport
TV was interesting	isn't interesting at all
winters were very cold	not very cold

Reading Corner

7. All of the following words have a small *ya, yu,* or *yo.* How would you write these words in *rōmaji*?

1. りょうり _____
2. かいしゃ _____
3. きょねん _____
4. せんしゅう _____
5. ひゃく _____

6. びょうき _____
7. ちゃいろ _____
8. じょうず _____
9. おきゃくさん _____
10. しゆみ _____

8. All of these words have a small *tsu,* which doubles the consonant that follows it. Match the beginnings and ends of the words, write the word in *rōmaji*, and then match it to its English meaning, as in the example.

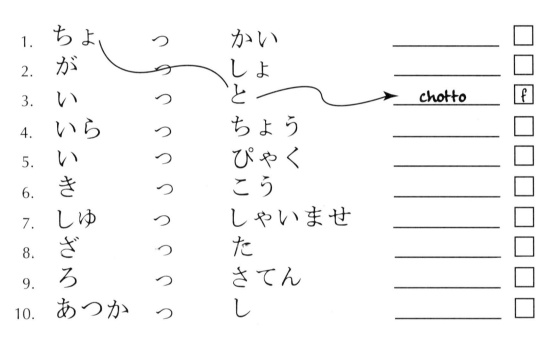

1. ちょ	っ	かい	_____ ☐
2. が	っ	しょ	_____ ☐
3. い	っ	と	chotto f
4. いら	っ	ちょう	_____ ☐
5. い	っ	ぴゃく	_____ ☐
6. き	っ	こう	_____ ☐
7. しゆ	っ	しゃいませ	_____ ☐
8. ざ	っ	た	_____ ☐
9. ろ	っ	さてん	_____ ☐
10. あつか	っ	し	_____ ☐

a. business trip	b. was hot	c. 1st floor	d. together	e. six hundred
f. a little	g. coffee shop	h. school	i. magazine	j. welcome

UNIT 10: Please wait over there.

In this unit, you'll practice making polite requests, responding to suggestions, giving directions, and describing the location of buildings.

Match Game

1. Please do it.

Match the sentence halves.

1. Kusuri o	( )	a. kiite kudasai.
2. Migi ni	( )	b. akete kudasai.
3. Jūsho o	( )	c. itte kudasai.
4. 7:00 ni	( )	d. nonde kudasai.
5. Eki no mae de	( )	e. kaite kudasai.
6. Watashi no hanashi o	( )	f. magatte kudasai.
7. Mado o	( )	g. matte kudasai.
8. Massugu	( )	h. kite kudasai.

Talking Point

2. The new coffee machine

Ms Hayashi has installed a new coffee machine in the coffee shop, and has just called over the staff to give them a demonstration. Fill in the missing lines from the ones given below to complete the conversation. (Be careful – there is one line too many.)

Hayashi Kore o mite kudasai. Atarashii kikai desu yo.

Kenji --

Hayashi --

Kenji --

Hayashi Sō desu. Ima kara tsukaimasu. Yoku mite kudasai. Mazu, koko ni mizu o irete kudasai.

Kenji --

Hayashi Kōhii wa, soko ni iremasu. Sore kara, kono botan o oshite kudasai. Sore dake desu.

Kenji --

Hayashi Go-fun gurai matte kudasai.

Kenji	-------------------------------------
Hayashi	Koko kara desu. Koppu o koko ni oite, sore kara kono akai botan o oshite kudasai. Wakarimashita ka. Ja, Matsuda san, dōzo.
Kenji	-------------------------------------
Hayashi	-------------------------------------
Kenji	Itai!!!

1. Dono gurai machimasu ka.
2. Hai. Mazu, kono botan o oshite ... Aa! Atsui! Atsui!
3. Subarashii desu ne. Nan desu ka.
4. Chigaimasu yo! Sono botan ja arimasen yo!
5. Hai. Kōhii wa?
6. Iie, kōhii wa oishii desu.
7. Kono kikai wa, totemo oishii kōhii o tsukurimasu yo. Demo atsui kara, ki o tsukete kudasai.
8. Kōhii wa doko kara demasu ka.
9. Hai, wakarimashita. Kyō kara tsukaimasu ka.

Language Focus

3. Where's the coffee shop?

Here's a description of the location of Kenji's coffee shop. Follow the route on the map, marking the various buildings mentioned, and finally where the coffee shop is. (Some of the buildings marked on the map are not mentioned.)

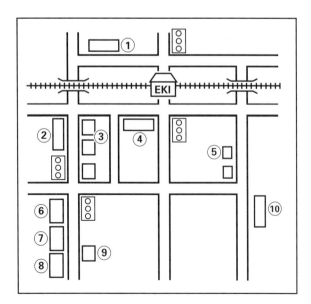

Eki o minami-guchi kara dete kudasai. Eki no mae ni shingō ga arimasu ga, sono shingō de migi ni magatte kudasai. Hidari-gawa ni eigakan ga arimasu. Sore kara, futatsu-me no kado o hidari ni magatte kudasai. Migi-gawa ni depāto ga atte, hidari-gawa ni iroiro-na resutoran ga arimasu. Tsugi no shingō de massugu itte kudasai. Migi-gawa ni ōkii tatemono ga arimasu. Sore wa ginkō desu. Sono ginkō to yūbinkyoku no aida ni, kissaten ga arimasu.

4. Polite requests

Susan is on her way to another interview by taxi. How does she ask the taxi driver to:

1. turn left at the next corner? _____

2. speak slowly? _____

3. go straight ahead? _____

4. close the window? _____

5. repeat what he said? _____

6. stop in front of that white building? _____

5. Responding to suggestions

Respond to the suggestions, as in the example.

> **Example:** Eigakan no naka de machimashō ka.
>
> (mae) **Iie, eigakan no mae de matte kudasai.** _____

1. **Q:** Ashita denwa shimashō ka.

   A: (kyō) _____

2. **Q:** Chikatetsu de ikimashō ka. _____

   A: (takushii) _____

3. **Q:** Hitotsu kaimashō ka. _____

   A: (futatsu) _____

4. **Q:** Wada san ni kikimashō ka. _____

   A: (Ishii san) _____

5. **Q:** Nihongo de hanashimashō ka. _____

   A: (Eigo) _____

6. **Q:** Ima tsukurimashō ka. _____

   A: (ato de) _____

6. Circle which of the following words is:

1. a part of the body

a. あした　　　　　b. ありました　　　　c. あたま　　　　　d. あつい

2. a color

a. くるま　　　　　b. くろい　　　　　c. くつ　　　　　d. くすり

3. a family member

a. ねこ　　　　　b. あの　　　　　c. きょねん　　　　d. あね

4. a means of transportation

a. ちかてつ　　　b. ちかいっかい　c. ちょと　　　　　d. ちがい

5. a building

a. もんだい　　　b. まっすぐ　　　c. ぎんこう　　　d. じかん

7. Choose the appropriate word to fill in the blanks. (All of the sentences are taken from this lesson.)

1. みぎに _____ ください。

a. まっすぐ　　b. まがって　　　c. みて　　　　d. のんで

2. _____ から、きをつけてください。

a. あき　　　　b. めかい　　　c. ひだい　　　d. あつい

3. つぎの _____ で、まっすぐいってください。

a. しんごう　　b. まど　　　　c. みぎ　　　　d. えいが

4. ちかてつで _____ か。

a. はなしましょう　b. いきましょう　c. つくりましょう　d. まがりま

5. ひだり _____ にえいがかんがあります。

a. ぎんこう　　b. あいだ　　　c. がっこう　　　d. がわ

UNIT 11: It's raining again.

In this unit, there are exercises to practice talking about what's happening at the moment, describing what someone is wearing, the weather, and making plans.

Match Game

1. The weather

Match the beginnings of the sentences to two suitable endings.

1. Ame ga futte imasu kara

2. Kyō wa ii tenki desu kara

3. Yuki ga futte imasu kara

4. Tsuyoi kaze ga fuite imasu kara

( ) a. kōto o kite, bōshi o kabutte kudasai.
( ) b. niwa ni suwatte imasu.
( ) c. ki o tsukete kudasai.
( ) d. niwa wa shiroku natte imasu.
( ) e. kasa wa dame desu.
( ) f. kasa o motte ikimashō.
( ) g. takushii de ikimashō.
( ) h. umi e ikimashō ka.

Talking Point

2. Kenji's waiting

Susan and her friend Makiko have finished classes for the day, and are about to leave the university to go home. Fill in the blanks either with the *-te imasu* form or the *-mashō* form of the given verb to complete their conversation.

Makiko   Iya-na tenki desu ne. Kasa o (motsu) _ _ _ _ _ _ _ _ _ _ _ _ _ _ ka.

Susan   Hai, (motsu) _ _ _ _ _ _ _ _ _ _ _ _ _ _ _ _ _ _ _ .

Makiko   Ja, (iku) _ _ _ _ _ _ _ _ _ _ _ _ _ _ _ _ _ _ .

Susan   Chotto matte kudasai ne. Ano hito wa mada soko ni (tatsu) _ _ _ _ _ _ _ _ _ _ _ _ _ _ _ ne.

Makiko   Dono hito desu ka. Doko?

Susan   Matsuda Kenji. Ano ki no shita ni (tatsu) _ _ _ _ _ _ _ _ _ _ _ _ _ _ _ _ yo. Kuroi bōshi o (kaburu) _ _ _ _ _ _ _ _ _ _ _ _ _ _ _ _ .

Makiko   Aa, akai kaban o (motsu) _ _ _ _ _ _ _ _ _ _ _ _ _ _ _ _ _ ne. Ano hito?

Susan	Sō desu.
Makiko	Ā, are wa Matsuda san desu ka. Sūzan san o (matsu) _____ ka.
Susan	Hai, sō omoimasu. Mainichi asoko de (matsu) _____. Iya desu.
Makiko	Sō desu ka. Ja, dō (suru) _____ ka. Ura no deguchi kara (deru) _____ ka.
Susan	Sō desu ne. Sō (suru) _____.

Word Power

3. What's Kenji wearing?

Look at the picture of Kenji, and write sentences about what he's wearing, using the verbs *kaburu, kiru, haku,* and *motte iru.*

Example: (jacket) **Kuroi jaketto o kite imasu.** _____

1. (hat) _____
2. (T-shirt) _____
3. (shirt) _____
4. (pants) _____
5. (sneakers) _____
6. (bag) _____

4. Missing vowels

Fill in the vowels to find out what the words are in each group.

Example: weather: m yk kz **ame yuki kaze**

1. clothes: skt kts ktssht zbn sts nkt

   ----

2. entertainment: rstrn knst ksstn g gkj

   ----

3. furniture: sf tbr trb s tsk

   ----

4. sports: tns grf s sk hkng skk

   ----

5. buildings: ybnkyk gnk gkk dpt gkn tshkn

(Picture labels: red, black, white, black, black, green, white)

Language Focus

5. The invitation

This morning Susan found a scribbled note from Makiko asking her if she'd like to go hiking tomorrow. Susan is about to call her to make arrangements to meet. What questions does she ask?

Example: (where go?) **Doko e ikimashō ka.**

1. (where meet?) _____
2. (what time meet?) _____
3. (what wear?) _____
4. (what take?) _____
5. (go by train?) _____

Sūzan san,
Ashita ii tenki deshō. Haikingu ni ikimashō ka. Konban denwa shite kudasai ne.

Makiko.

6. Word order

Rearrange the groups of words to make questions or sentences.
(Be careful – there is one word too many in each group.)

1. eki/aimashō/nan-ji/de/ashita/o/ni/ka

10:00 wa dō desu ka.

2. Sūzan/haite/sukāto/o/wa/kite/kuroi/imasu/san/ka

Iie, kyō wa wanpiisu o kite imasu.

3. kara/takushii/kaerimashō/ame/kaze/imasu/de/ga/futte/ka

Hai, sō shimashō.

4. nani/tabete/imasu/dō shite/imasen/mo/ka

O-naka ga chotto itai kara desu.

5. kaze/tsukete/tsuyoi/o/ga/kudasai/ni/kara/ki/

Hai, wakarimashita.

Reading Corner

7. This section introduces the first 10 *katakana* characters. Match the characters to their sounds.

1. ギ 2. ア 3. イ 4. コ
5. ク 6. カ 7. エ
8. ゴ 9. ウ 10. キ 11. ガ
12. グ 14. オ
13. ケ 15. ゲ

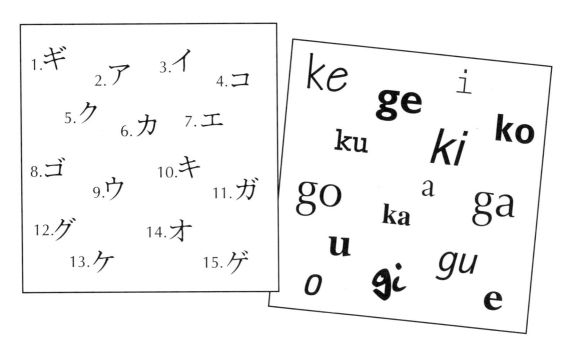

ke   i
ge
ku   ki   ko
go   a
ka   ga
u
o   gi   gu   e

8. Write the following words in *rōmaji,* and then guess what the meaning might be before checking the answers. Remember that a line (–) between characters lengthens the previous vowel sound.

	rōmaji	meaning
1. ケーキ	_____	_____
2. ココア	_____	_____
3. コーク	_____	_____
4. オーケー	_____	_____
5. カーキ	_____	_____

UNIT 12: Review

1. Matching

Match the sentences which have a similar meaning.

1. Amari genki ja arimasen.
2. Ani to imōto to watashi desu.
3. Supōtsu wa kirai desu.
4. Eiga wa nagakatta desu.
5. Shigoto wa totemo isogashii desu.
6. Jū-has-sai ni narimashita.
7. Igirisujin desu.
8. Konban dekakemasen.

(   ) a. Rondon ni sunde imasu.
(   ) b. Uchi de terebi o mimasu.
(   ) c. Doyōbi mo kaisha ni ikimasu.
(   ) d. O-naka ga chotto itai desu.
(   ) e. Mō kodomo ja arimasen.
(   ) f. Roku-ji kara ku-ji made deshita.
(   ) g. Kodomo san-nin desu.
(   ) h. Suiei mo tenisu mo zenzen dame desu.

2. A, B, or C?

Choose the most appropriate answer to each question.

1. O-genki desu ka.
   a. Hai, sumimasen.
   b. Arigatō.
   c. Hai, o-kage sama de.

2. Iya-na tenki desu ne.
   a. Sō, ii desu ne.
   b. Ē, yuki wa kirai desu ne.
   c. Yuki ga suki desu ka.

3. Moshi moshi.
   a. Tanaka san desu.
   b. Moshi moshi.
   c. Dare desu ka.

4. O-niisan no namae wa nan desu ka.
   a. Kenji desu.
   b. Kenji san desu.
   c. Matsuda san desu.

5. Densha de ikimashō ka.
   a. Ikimashō.
   b. Hai, ikimashita.
   c. Iie, takushii de ikimashō.

6. Ano eiga wa dō deshita ka.
   a. Amari omoshiroku nakatta desu yo.
   b. Iie, yoku arimasen deshita.
   c. Ii eiga desu.

3. Find the word

Each word below has **-ari-** in it. Look at the clues and complete the words.

1. next to   _ _ _ a r i
2. I see, got it   _ _ _ a r i _ _ _ _ _ _ _
3. not much   _ _ a r i
4. thank you   a r i _ _ _ _

5. two people   _ _ _ a r i
6. left   _ _ _ a r i
7. turn   _ _ _ a r i _ _ _ _
8. become   _ a r i _ _ _ _

4. -masu forms and -te forms

Complete this chart with the appropriate -te forms and -masu forms.

	-masu	-te
1.	nomimasu	
2.		tabete
3.	ikimasu	
4.		natte
5.		katte
6.	aimasu	
7.		hanashite
8.	kikimasu	
9.	yomimasu	
10.		matte

5. Instructions

Give instructions to go with each of the pictures.

Example: _Shingō de migi ni magatte kudasai._

1. _____
2. _____
3. _____
4. _____
5. _____
6. _____

1.

2.

3.

4.

5.

6.

50

6. Crossword

Find the missing words from the sentences below to complete the crossword.

Across:

5. Kinō _ _ _ _ _ sūtsu o kaimashita yo. Takakatta!

7. Koko _ _ _ _ _ oite kudasai.

8. Mensetsu wa _ _ _ _ _ deshita ka.

9. Natsu wa suki desu ga, _ _ _ _ _ wa amari suki ja arimasen.

10. _ _ _ _ _ 11:00 ni nemasu.

12. _ _ _ _ _ ni magatte kudasai.

13. Hidari ja arimasen. _ _ _ _ _ desu.

14. Ii tenki desu kara, haha wa _ _ _ _ _ ni suwatte imasu.

16. Sono hanashi ga wakarimasen deshita. Mō ichido _ _ _ _ _ kudasai.

17. Konsāto wa 10:15 _ _ _ _ _ desu.

18. Kono kusuri o _ _ _ _ _ kudasai.

19. Sore o doko _ _ _ _ _ kaimashita ka.

Down:

1. Kyō wa getsuyōbi ja arimasen yo. _ _ _ _ _ desu.

2. Sumimasen ga, eigo ga _ _ _ _ _ .

3. Sūzan san no _ _ _ _ _ wa haikingu to ongaku desu.

4. Nihongo no kurasu no hito wa _ _ _ _ _ Igirisujin desu ka.

6. Matsuda san no kaisha wa doko ni_ _ _ _ _ ka.

11. Sore wa doko kara _ _ _ _ _ tokei desu ka.

12. Kissaten wa eki no _ _ _ _ _ guchi ni arimasu.

15. Ushiro no deguchi kara _ _ _ _ _ kudasai.

16. Furansugo? _ _ _ _ _ , dekimasen.

7. Categories

Put the remaining words with the appropriate group.

> imōto takushii furui minami doko haha atarashii chairo orenji
> higashi dore kuruma mazui midori ōtobai shujin dare

1. akai   murasaki   _____

2. musuko   ani   _____

3. densha   hikōki   _____

4. dō shite   nani   _____

5. kita   nishi   _____

6. hayai   atsui   _____

8. What did they do?

Look at the chart, and write sentences about what Katō san and Itō san did and didn't do last week.

	Katō	Satō
play tennis	✔	✗
see a movie	✔	✔
1. did the shopping	✔	✔
2. went to Yokohama	✔	✗
3. went out last night	✔	✔
4. studied English	✗	✗
5. ate at a Spanish restaurant	✔	✗
6. read the paper every day	✔	✗

Example: Katō san wa tenisu o shimashita ga, Satō san wa shimasen deshita. Katō san mo Satō san mo eiga o mimashita.

1. _____
2. _____
3. _____
4. _____
5. _____
6. _____

9. Read the following and answer the questions.

きのうはにちようびでした。あさからあめがふっていましたから、どこへもいきませんでした。ケーキをつくりましたが、ぜんぜんおいしくなかったです。そのあとえいごのべんきょうをすこししましたが、とてもむずかしかったから、よくできませんでした。よるにともだちにでんわをしましたが、だれもいませんでした。あまりいいいちにちじゃありませんでした。

1. How was the weather yesterday? _____

2. What did this person make yesterday? _____

3. How were they? _____

4. What was difficult? _____

5. What did this person do in the evening? _____

UNIT 13: What does he look like?

In this unit, you'll practice describing people, using several adjectives together, and making comparisons.

Match Game

1. Who's who?

Match the descriptions to the appropriate pictures.

1. se ga takai
2. se ga hikui
3. yasete imasu
4. futotte imasu
5. wakai
6. toshi o totte imasu
7. kami ga kuroi
8. kami ga usui

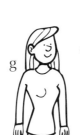

Talking Point

2. The second interview

Kenji went for another job interview yesterday, and Ms Hayashi at the coffee shop is asking him how it went. Read through their conversation, and then see if the statements which follow are true or false.

Hayashi Mata mensetsu ga arimashita ne. Dō deshita ka.

Kenji Taihen deshita!

Hayashi Dō shite desu ka. Shitsumon ga muzukashikatta kara?

Kenji Iie, shitsumon wa kantan deshita ga, kowai hito ga imashita yo.

Kenji *(laughing)* Kowai hito? Dō iu imi desu ka. Donna hito?

Hayashi Yo-nin imashita ga, hitori dake shitsumon o shimashita. Sono hito wa onna no hito deshita. Namae wa Obata san.

Hayashi Sorede?

Kenji Kowai hito deshita yo. Se ga takakute, kami no ke ga mijikakute, totemo yasete iru hito deshita. Kuroi sūtsu o kite imashita. Sore kara totemo kibishii kao o shite imashita yo. Zenzen shinsetsu ja arimasen deshita.

53

Hayashi	Sō desu ka. Ja, kono mae no mensetsu no hō ga umaku ikimashita ne.
Kenji	Sō desu ne. Kinō no mensetsu yori zutto yokatta.

1. Kinō no mensetsu no shitsumon wa taihen deshita.	*True/False*
2. Kowai hito wa onna no hito deshita.	*True/False*
3. Yo-nin no hito ga minna iroiro-na shitsumon o shimashita.	*True/False*
4. Onna no hito wa zenzen waraimasen deshita.	*True/False*
5. Obata san wa futotte imasen deshita.	*True/False*
6. Mae no mensetsu no hō ga yokatta desu.	*True/False*

 # Word Power

3. What a face!

Can you name these parts of the body?

1. _ _ _ _ _ _ _ _ _ _
2. _ _ _ _ _ _ _ _ _ _
3. _ _ _ _ _ _ _ _ _ _
4. _ _ _ _ _ _ _ _ _ _
5. _ _ _ _ _ _ _ _ _ _
6. _ _ _ _ _ _ _ _ _ _
7. _ _ _ _ _ _ _ _ _ _
8. _ _ _ _ _ _ _ _ _ _

 # Language Focus

4. Comparisons

Susan and her friend Makiko are similar in some ways, but different in others. Make comparisons between them, using the following information.

	SUSAN	MAKIKO
height	5'7"	5'5"
1. **hair**	short	long
2. **age**	25	22
3. **weight**	147 lb	138 lb
4. **study**	works most evenings	doesn't work in evenings
5. **boyfriends**	none	lots
6. **good at sports**	yes	so-so

Example: (taller) _Sūzan san wa, Makiko san yori se ga takai desu._

1. (longer hair) _____
2. (older) _____
3. (slimmer) _____
4. (works harder) _____
5. (more boyfriends) _____
6. (better at sports) _____

5. Word order

Put the words in the correct order to make questions, and then answer the questions.

1. no/to/to/chairo/dochira no hō/desu/aoi/me/me/ga/suki/ka

   Q: _____ A: _____

2. ga/dochira no hō/furui/Tōkyō/Kyōto/desu/to/to/ka

   Q: _____ A: _____

3. ga/ga/ame/desu/dochira no hō/ōi/fuyu/aki/to/to/ka

   Q: _____ A: _____

4. yoku/bideo/o/dochira no hō/mimasu/terebi/to/to/ka

   Q: _____ A: _____

5. sakana/tabemasu/yoku/niku/to/o/to/dochira no hō/ka

   Q: _____ A: _____

6. Describing people

Susan has received a lot of business cards since she's been in Japan, and to make sure she remembers who's who, she always scribbles some details about each person on the card after she gets home. Look at the cards, and write sentences like the one in the example.

FUJIMI BANK

TOSHIO ISHII
Chief Accountant

1st Floor Tokyo Kosto Kaian
Yurakucho Chiyoda-ku Tokyo
Tel: (03) 3221-4182

Long hair, Elderly

Example: _Ishii san wa, kami no ke ga nagakute, toshi o totte imasu._

1. TOKYO NEWS SERVICE

Black hair, Blue eyes

Tim Carter
Reporter
7th Floor Tokyo Kosts, Kailan
Shimuku-ku Yotsuya, Tokyo
Tel (03)8556-3259. Fax (03)8569 1548

MATSUDA DEPARTMENT STORE

Yumi Kubota

1 Ichiban-cho,
Chiyoda-ku, Tokyo
Tel (03) 3221-4182. Fax (03) 3265-5511

2. *Tall, Slim*

3. KKo Co. Ltd

Hair thinning, glasses

ICHIRO YAMAGUCHI
Sales Manager
7th Floor, Tokyo Kosts, Kailan, Shimuku-ku Yotsuya, Tokyo
Tel (03)8556-3259. Fax (03)8569 1548

4. YAMAICHI UNIVERSITY

Large eyes, Fat!

YASUHIRO HONDA
ASSISTANT PROFESSOR
10-1 Yurakucho 2-chome
Chiyoda-ku Tokyo
Tel (03) 3221-4182

5. J.B. ENGINEERING

Sue Rogers
120-126 Top Floor Tokyo Kosts Ka
Shimuku-ku Yotsuya Tokyo
Tel (03)6993-3259
Fax (03)6933-1526

Young, Short hair

1. _____
2. _____
3. _____
4. _____
5. _____

Reading Corner

7. The *katakana* characters for *sa, shi, su, se,* and *so* are introduced in this unit. Write the *rōmaji* equivalent by the side of each character.

1. セ _____
2. ザ _____
3. ゾ _____
4. シ _____

5. ジ _____
6. ズ _____
7. サ _____

8. ス _____
9. ソ _____
10. ゼ _____

8. Circle the word which has the pronunciation given at the beginning of the line, and then guess what the word might be in English.

1. Shikago   a. ジガコ   b. シカゴ   c. シガコ   d. スケゴ   _____

2. uisukii   a. ウイースキ   b. アイスキー   c. ウエスキー   d. ウイスキー   _____

3. sākasu   a. サーカス   b. サカース   c. サガス   d. セーカス   _____

4. sōsēji   a. ゾーセジ   b. ソーセージ   c. スースージ   d. サーセージー   _____

5. kōsu   a. カース   b. コーズ   c. コース   d. キース   _____

UNIT 14: On the train

In this unit, you'll practice the plain form of verbs. You'll also practice talking about things you can and can't do, joining sentences with "but" and "because," and saying what you are thinking about.

Match Game

1. So/because

Match the halves of the sentences, joining them with *kara*.

1. Ame ga futte iru	kara	a. takushii de ikimashō.
2. Nihongo ga dekinai	kara	b. Higashiyama eki ni wa tomarimasen.
3. Kono seki ga aite iru	kara	c. kasa o motte itte kudasai.
4. Hikōki ga suki ja nai	kara	d. eigo de hanashite kudasai.
5. Sumimasen, yoku wakaranai	kara	e. dōzo suwatte kudasai.
6. Nimotsu ga omoi	kara	f. Shinkansen de Kyūshu e ikimashita.
7. Kyūkō da	kara	g. mō ichido setsumei shite kudasai.

Talking Point

2. Chance encounter

Susan is travelling down to Osaka to visit some friends, and has just come back from the restaurant car on the Shinkansen (Bullet Train) to find somebody sitting in the seat next to hers. As she sits down, he speaks to her. Fill in each blank with the *-masu* form of one of the verbs given below given in their plain form.

Passenger *(hesitantly)* Shitsurei desu ga, nihongo ga _____ ka.

Susan Hai, sukoshi _____ ga.

Passenger *(embarrassed)* Jitsu wa, boku no pen wa soko ni _____ ga ...

Susan Nan desu ka? Chotto _____ ga. Pen desu ka. Anata no pen?

Passenger Hai. Sono seki no ue desu. Anata wa watashi no pen no ue ni suwatte

_____.

Susan E? Pen no ue ni? Sumimasen ne! *(standing up and finding the pen on her seat)* Ā, koko ni _____ ne. Dōzo.

> aru x 2
> iku x 2
> wakaranai
> iru x 2
> dekiru x 2
> inai
> ja nai

57

Passenger Dōmo sumimasen. Jitsu wa, sono seki ni dare mo suwatte _____ to omoimashita kara ...

Susan Ii desu yo.

Passenger Shitsurei desu ga, dochira made _____ ka. Kyōto?

Susan Iie, Kyōto _____. Ōsaka made _____. Tomodachi ga Ōsaka ni sunde _____ kara.

Word Power

3. Train travel

Complete these sentences to find out what the stranger on the train is thinking about Susan.

1. Tōkyō kara Nagoya made — de ikimashita.

2. Ōfuku desu ka. Iie, — desu.

3. Kyōto made nan-jikan — n' desu ka.

4. Sumimasen ga, kono — wa aite imasu ka.

5. Jiyūseki desu ka. Iie, — desu.

6. Ōsaka-yuki wa san-ban- — kara desu.

7. Densha ga 3-ban hōmu kara 4:30 ni — shimasu.

8. Eki no minami- — de aimashō.

9. Kippu o nan- — kaimashita ka.

10. Kodomo ni-mai to — ichi-mai kudasai.

11. Rasshu no densha wa taihen — imasu ne.

4. Definitions

Which is the correct definition of each word?

1. **kyūkō:**
   a. yoku tomaru densha
   b. amari tomaranai densha
   c. Shinkansen

2. **baiten:**
   a. chiisai mise
   b. kippu uriba
   c. tabemono

3. **nimotsu:**
   a. kaban to sūtsukēsu
   b. tabemono to nomimono
   c. eki no hitotachi

4. **tabi:**
   a. kutsu
   b. basu
   c. ryokō

5. **shokudō-sha:**
   a. totemo ōkii kuruma
   b. densha no naka no resutoran
   c. osoi densha

Language Focus

5. I can't swim!

Put a check (✓) or a cross (✗) against the things you can and can't do, then write sentences about yourself.

Example: Kanji o kaku koto ga dekimasen.

1. _____
2. _____
3. _____
4. _____
5. _____
6. _____
7. _____

> write *kanji* ✗
> 1. read *hiragana*
> 2. get up early in the morning
> 3. speak French
> 4. eat raw fish *(sashimi)*
> 5. make cakes
> 6. swim
> 7. sing well

6. *kara* or *kedo*?

Join the sentences with *kara* or *kedo*, as appropriate.

Example: Kyō wa doyōbi desu. Shinkansen ga konde imasu.

Kyō wa doyōbi da kara, shinkansen ga konde imasu.

1. Hikōki ga kowai desu. Itsumo densha ka kuruma de ryokō shimasu.

_____

2. Itō san mo watashitachi to issho ni kimasu. Kippu o san-mai katte kudasai.

_____

3. Kanji o yomu koto ga dekimasu. Kaku koto wa dekimasen.

_____

4. Densha wa 8:30 ni shuppatsu shimasu. 8:15 made ni eki e kite kudasai.

_____

5. Mainichi benkyō shimasu. Zenzen jōzu ni narimasen.

_____

6. Kyō wa ame ga futte imasu. Basu wa osoi desu.

_____

59

7. What is she thinking?

During a pause in conversation while the stranger goes to get some drinks, Susan sits staring out of the window. What is she thinking?

Example: Se ga takakute, hansamu da to omotte imasu.

1. _____

2. _____

3. _____

4. _____

5. _____

tall and handsome!

1. carrying a very expensive briefcas

2. isn't married!!

3. lives in Tokyo

4. can speak a little English

5. wearing an expensive suit

Reading Corner

8. Match the *katakana* characters to their *rōmaji* equivalents.

1. チ　2. ダ　3. ド
4. テ　　5. ヅ
6. ヂ　7. タ　8. ツ
9. デ　10. ト

de　　ta　zu
　chi
te　　ji　do
　　tsu
da　　　to

9. Find the *katakana* equivalents of the following words.

1. guitar	2. sweater	3. test	4. Germany	5. cheese
6. toast	7. suit	**8. taxi**	9. dessert	10. soda

ターアオ⦅タクシー⦆キウテストーストチーソーダイエドイツ
オカスーツセーターギシーデザートドスチーズタゴギターア

UNIT 15: Are you free tonight?

In this unit, you'll practice making and responding to invitations. You'll also practice dates, reported speech, and the plain form of verbs in the past tense.

Match Game

1. Invitations

Match the invitations or comments on the left with an appropriate response from the right.

1. Doyōbi ni, yakyū o mi ni ikimasen ka.

2. Konban wa aite imasu ka.

3. Sumimasen ga, 31-nichi wa chotto isogashii desu.

4. Watashi no tanjōbi no pātii ni kimasen ka.

5. Eki no mae de 7:30 ni aimashō ka.

6. Nichiyōbi, doraibu ni ikimasen ka.

7. Konban karaoke bā ni ikimasen ka.

( ) a. Ē, sō shimashō.

( ) b. Ii desu ne. Arigatō. Itsu desu ka.

( ) c. Watashi wa uta ga amari jōzu ja nai n' desu yo!

( ) d. Sō desu ka. Zannen desu ne.

( ) e. Hai, aite imasu yo. Nanika ...?

( ) f. Zannen desu ga, doyōbi wa chotto ...

( ) g. Ii desu ne. Doko e?

Talking Point

2. The invitation

Now, back in Tokyo, Susan gets a phone call from the man on the train, with whom she exchanged name cards. Fill in his lines from those given below to find out what he says.

Susan	Moshi moshi. Kūpā desu.
Ikeda	---
Susan	Ā, Ikeda san. Hai, yoku oboete imasu. Anō ... shutchō wa ikaga deshita ka.
Ikeda	---
Susan	Ē, tanoshikatta desu. Iroiro-na koto o shimashita.
Ikeda	---

Susan	Iie, ikimasen deshita. Jikan ga arimasen deshita kara.
Ikeda	--
Susan	Hai?
Ikeda	--
Susan	Doyōbi desu ka. Sore wa 13-nichi desu ne. Hai, aite iru to omoimasu ga.
Ikeda	--

1. Sore wa zannen deshita ne. Anō, tokorode, jitsu wa ...

2. Arigatō, umaku ikimashita. Kūpā san wa? Shūmatsu wa dō deshita ka. Tanoshikatta desu ka.

3. Raishū no doyōbi wa aite iru deshō ka.

4. Moshi moshi. Kūpā san? Kochira wa Ikeda desu. Senshū Shinkansen no naka de atta Ikeda desu.

5. Jitsu wa, "Cabaret" to iu myūjikāru o mi ni ikimasu ga, Sūzan san wa issho ni ikimasen ka.

6. Kyōto wa? Ikimashita ka.

Word Power

3. Dates

Fill in the missing dates.

1st	tsuitachi	8th	-----------------	15th	-----------------
2nd	futsuka	9th	-----------------	16th	-----------------
3rd	-----------------	10th	tōka	17th	-----------------
4th	-----------------	11th	-----------------	18th	-----------------
5th	-----------------	12th	-----------------	19th	jū-ku-nichi
6th	-----------------	13th	jū-san-nichi	20th	-----------------
7th	nanoka	14th	-----------------	21st	ni-jū-ichi-nichi

4. How about going to …

Below are some places or events you might receive an invitation to or visit by yourself.
Add vowels to find out what each word is, and match it to the equivalent English meaning.

Example: kbk – *kabuki (Japanese traditional theater)*

1. knst _____
2. hkbtskn _____
3. jnj _____
4. bjtskn _____
5. nsn _____
6. tr _____
7. gkj _____
8. drb _____

hot springs

museum

concert

shrine

a drive

art gallery

temple

theater

Language Focus

5. Refusing invitations

You are trying to find time to get together with a friend. Look at the calendar, and respond to the invitations by
explaining what you are doing at that time.

MAY						
Mon	Tue	Wed	Thur	Fri	Sat	Sun
3 9.15 DENTIST! 6.30–8.30 Japanese class	4 10.00 – Japanese test p.m. LECTURES	5 p.m. Yokohama 6.30 Japanese class	6 Mother's Birthday	7 part-time job 5.30 DOCTOR	8 hiking in Japan Alps	9

Example: Getsuyōbi no yoru wa dō desu ka. *Zannen desu ga, getsuyōbi no yoru wa nihongo no kurasu ga aru n' desu.*

1. Yokka no asa wa dō desu ka. _____
2. Suiyōbi no gogo wa dō desu ka. _____
3. Mokuyōbi wa ikaga desu ka. _____
4. Nanoka wa dō desu ka. _____
5. Yōka ka kokonoka wa ikaga desu ka. _____

63

6. Find the dialogue

Choose which response is appropriate to make a conversation.

Doyōbi wa aite imasu ka.

A. Sō desu ne. Bōringu wa dō deshita ka.
B. Sō desu ne. Bōringu wa dō desu ka.

A. Sō desu ka. Ja, doraibu wa?
B. Watashi mo suki desu ne.

A. Hai, aite imasu yo. Dokoka e ikimashō ka.
B. Hai, chotto isogashii desu.

A. Bōringu wa amari suki ja nai n' desu ga ...
B. Bōringu ni ikimasen ka.

A. Zannen desu ne. Doraibu ni ikimashō.
B. Ii desu ne. Doraibu ni ikimashō.

Reading Corner

7. Circle the *katakana* characters for *na, ni, nu, ne,* and *no.*

1. ア	2. ナ	3. ク	4. ニ	5. タ	6. ノ
7. ネ	8. ヌ	9. ソ	10. ツ	11. ウ	12. ス

8. Write out the following words in *rōmaji*, and then match them to their English equivalents.

1. カナダ ＿＿＿＿＿ a. nude
2. カヌー ＿＿＿＿＿ b. night game (baseball)
3. テニス ＿＿＿＿＿ c. necktie
4. ヌード ＿＿＿＿＿ d. nougat
5. ネクタイ ＿＿＿＿＿ e. casino
6. ネガ ＿＿＿＿＿ f. Canada
7. ノート ＿＿＿＿＿ g. canoe
8. ナイター ＿＿＿＿＿ h. note, notebook
9. ヌーガ ＿＿＿＿＿ i. tennis
10. カジノ ＿＿＿＿＿ j. negative

UNIT 16: You'd better go home.

In this unit, you'll practice giving advice, using informal levels of speech, saying what you do and don't want to do, naming parts of the body, and explaining how you don't feel well.

Match Game

1. I'm not well.

Match the sentences to the appropriate pictures.

1. Ha ga itai n' desu.
2. Atama ga itai n' desu.
3. Kaze o hiita n' desu.
4. Netsu ga aru n' desu.
5. Nodo ga itai n' desu.
6. Seki ga deru n' desu.
7. O-naka ga itai n' desu.

Talking Point

2. What happened?

Susan meets up with Makiko after the last class of the day. Read through their conversation, and then see if the statements which follow are true, false, or not mentioned in the dialogue.

Makiko	Dō shita n' desu ka. Genki ga nai wa ne.
Susan	Ē. Atama ga itakute, o-naka mo itai n' desu. Sore kara kinō no yoru, neru koto ga dekinakatta no.
Makiko	Ara, dō shita n' desu ka. Kaze? Uchi e kaette, hayaku neta hō ga ii n' ja nai?
Susan	Sō da kedo, 7:30 ni yakusoku ga aru kara ...
Makiko	Kenji san ni au n' desu ka.
Susan	*(angrily)* Iie, Kenji san ja nai n' desu yo. Kenji san ni wa mō zenzen aitaku nai no.
Makiko	Dō shite?

Susan   Kenji san no sei da yo. Daiji-na hanashi ga aru to kare ga itte ita kara, issho ni tabe ni itta ne. Totemo ii resutoran da to kiite ita kedo, chiisakute, kitanai tokoro datta. Tabemono mo totemo mazukatta. Takushii de uchi e kaetta kedo, takushii no naka de byōki ni natta yo.

Makiko   Sō desu ka. Ja, sono daiji-na hanashi wa?

Susan   Nakatta! Watashi to issho ni sono resutoran e ikitakatta dake da to itta!

1. Sūzan san wa ima kimochi ga warui desu.	*True/False/NM*
2. Sūzan san wa kesa hayaku okimashita.	*True/False/NM*
3. Makiko san wa, Sūzan san wa hayaku kaetta hō ga ii to omotte imasu.	*True/False/NM*
4. Kinō no yoru, Sūzan san wa Kenji san to issho ni totemo ii resutoran ni ikimashita.	*True/False/NM*
5. Kaeri no takushii wa jikan ga kakarimashita.	*True/False/NM*
6. Kenji san wa daiji-na hanashi ga arimashita.	*True/False/NM*

Word Power

3. Parts of the body

Unscramble the letters to find the names of parts of the body, and then mark them on the picture.

1. due   ----------------------------------
2. hais   ----------------------------------
3. et   ----------------------------
4. atak   ----------------------------------
5. haiz   ----------------------------------
6. buyi   ----------------------------------
7. kaaon   ----------------------------------
8. sokhi   ----------------------------------
9. buketi   ----------------------------------

4. When I'm tired ...

Complete the sentences with an appropriate word or phrase from the box.

1. _____ toki ni, tomodachi ni denwa shimasu.
2. _____ toki ni, hayaku nemasu.
3. _____ toki ni, mizu ya jūsu o nomimasu.
4. _____ toki ni, chiizu sando to ka tabemasu.
5. _____ toki ni, haisha ni ikimasu.
6. _____ toki ni, kao ga akaku narimasu.
7. _____ toki ni, sētā o kimasu.
8. _____ toki ni, megane o kakemasu.

> tsukareta
> ha ga itai
> samui
> nodo ga kawaita
> me ga itai
> sabishii
> hazukashii
> onaka ga suita

Language Focus

5. Giving advice

What kind of advice would you give if you heard these comments from your friends? Using the cues, make sentences like the one in the example.

Example: Ha ga itai! (go to the dentist) *Haisha ni itta hō ga ii desu yo.*

1. Me ga itai yo. (wear your glasses) _____
2. Samui! (wear that sweater) _____
3. Kimochi ga warui yo. (go home early) _____
4. Mata seki ga deru ne. (quit smoking cigarettes) _____
5. Kaze o hiita to omou yo. (take some medicine) _____

6. I want to ...

Although she's still not feeling very well, Susan makes it to her date with the man from the train, Shūsaku Ikeda. At the restaurant, they talk about what they would like to do if they had a lot of money. Write sentences like the one in the example about what each of them does and doesn't want to do.

Example: (live in the country) *Sūzan san wa inaka ni sumitai kedo, Ikeda san wa inaka ni sumitaku arimasen.*

	SUSAN	IKEDA
live in the country	✔	✘
quit work	✔	✔
1. study French	✔	✔
2. go to Africa	✔	✘
3. buy a large car	✘	✘
4. get up late every morning	✔	✔
5. stay in expensive hotels	✔	✘

(quit work) *Sūzan san mo Ikeda san mo shigoto o yametai desu.*

1. _____

2. _____

3. _____

4. _____

5. _____

Reading Corner

7. Write the *rōmaji* equivalent next to each *katakana* character.

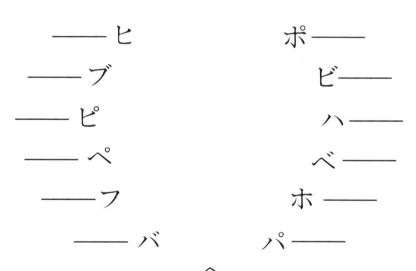

—— ヒ   ポ ——

—— ブ   ビ ——

—— ピ   ハ ——

—— ペ   ベ ——

—— フ   ホ ——

—— バ   パ ——

ヘ
——

8. Circle the word in *katakana* which is the equivalent of the word given at the beginning of the line.

1. passport	a. パースポト	b. パスホート	c. パスポート	d. パスホオト
2. souvenir	a. スーベニア	b. スーベニーア	c. スーノニー	d. スーノニア
3. business	a. ビズネス	b. ビズネイス	c. ブジネス	d. ビジネス
4. knife	a. ニーフ	b. ナイフ	c. カナーフ	d. ナーヘ
5. know-how	a. ノハウ	b. ノーホー	c. ノーハウ	d. ノーハー
6. piano	a. ピアノ	b. ビアノ	c. ピーアノ	d. ピアノー

UNIT 17: May I?

In this unit, you'll practice asking for and giving permission, and talking about your plans and intentions.

Match Game

1. May I?

Match the requests for permission on the left to appropriate responses on the right.

1. Denwa o tsukatte mo ii desu ka.
2. Mado o shimete mo ii desu ka.
3. Koko ni suwatte mo ii desu ka.
4. Kore o tabenakute mo ii desu ka.
5. Kono shimbun o yonde mo ii desu ka.
6. Sumimasen, tabako o sutte mo ii desu ka.
7. Shashin o totte mo ii desu ka.
8. Ashita no kaigi ni denakute mo ii desu ka.

( ) a. Sumimasen ga, aite imasen.
( ) b. Iie, hazukashii yo!
( ) c. Watashi no shimbun ja nai n' desu.
( ) d. Dōzo dōzo, tsukatte kudasai.
( ) e. Deta hō ga ii to omoimasu yo.
( ) f. Ii desu yo. Chotto samui desu ne.

( ) g. Iie, tabete kudasai yo.
( ) h. Iie, koko de wa tabako o sutte wa ikemasen.

Talking Point

2. A business trip

Mrs Matsuda and her colleague, Shūsaku Ikeda, (yes, the man on the train) are going on a business trip to Sendai next week, and she is just confirming the plans with Ms Okada in the Sendai office. Put the sentences in the correct order to read their conversation. The first sentence is marked for you.

1. _____ Taihen desu ne! Ato Tōkyō kara dareka kimasu ka.

2. _____ Wakarimashita. Ikeda kachō wa? Issho ni getsuyōbi no yoru kuru n' desu ka.

3. _____ Ē, sono hō ga ii desu ne. Hoteru no yoyaku wa? Kochira de shimashō ka.

4. _____ Iie, getsuyōbi no yoru, Tōkyō de dareka to au yotei ga aru to iimashita. Dakara kayōbi no asa hayaku okite, Sendai ni iku tsumori da to omou n' desu ga.

5. _____ Iie, watashitachi futari dake desu.

6. __1__ Itsu kimasu ka. Kayōbi no asa desu ka.

7. _____ Iie, shinakute mo ii desu. Sendai ni sunde iru tomodachi ga iru kara, sono tomodachi no uchi ni tomaru tsumori desu.

8. _____ Iie, mae no ban ni iku tsumori desu. Kaigi wa asa 9:30 kara deshō? Dakara getsuyōbi no yoru itta hō ga ii to omoimasu.

Word Power

3. Something and nothing

Complete these sentences with *nanika, nanimo, dareka, daremo,* or *dokoka*.

1. Sumimasen ga, kachō wa _____ e dekakemashita.

2. Kinō onaka ga itakatta kara, _____ tabemasen deshita.

3. _____ inakatta kara, taihen sabishikatta desu.

4. Sūzan san wa _____ to issho ni eiga o mi ni itta deshō?

5. Biiru ka _____ nomimashō ka.

6. Iroiro-na tomodachi ni denwa shita kedo, _____ imasen deshita.

7. Okane ga nai kara, _____ dekimasen.

8. Raishū no doyōbi ni de mo mata _____ de aimashō yo.

4. Don't do that!

Look at the signs in the art gallery, and complete them by writing in an appropriate verb from those given below. (There are three extra verbs given.)

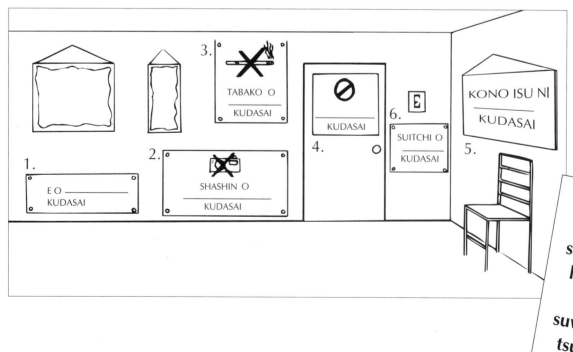

suwanaide
shinaide
sawaranaide
hairanaide
konaide
suwaranaide
tsukenaide
toranaide
minaide

Language Focus

5. Susan's plans

Susan is busy, and her diary is filling up. Make sentences about her plans, referring to the diary below.

Example: (6th) _Muika no yoru, Shūsaku san to nomi ni iku yotei desu._

1. (7th) _____

2. (8th) _____

3. (9th) _____

4. (9th) _____

5. (10th) _____

6. (11th) _____

MONDAY 6th
evening ~ go for drink with Shūsaku!

TUESDAY 7th
p.m. ~ teach English to Mrs Hirota in Kawasaki

WEDNESDAY 8th
a.m. ~ DENTIST!

THURSDAY 9th
morning ~ attend meeting of hiking club
evening ~ go and see French film with Makiko

FRIDAY 10th
p.m. ~ go to Yokohama, stay over at Makiko's

SATURDAY 11th
p.m. ~ go to Ginza (buy new shoes & dress)

6. Rules of the house

Susan is going to live in the university dormitory for the last few months of the term, and she has to find out the rules. Here's a list of things she asked about, with a check (✔) for those things allowed in the rooms, and a cross (✗) for those that are not. Write sentences using _-te mo ii desu_ or _-te wa ikemasen_ as in the example.

is it okay to –

Example: cook?   ✔ _Ryōri o shite mo ii desu._

1. listen to music?   ✔ _____

2. smoke?   ✔ _____

3. keep _(kau)_ pets?   ✗ _____

4. have parties?   ✗ _____

5. drink alcohol?   ✔ _____

6. come back late in the evening?   ✗ _____

7. Word order

Put the words into the correct order to make questions, and then answer the questions.

1. tsumori/kaimono/iku/ashita/desu/ni/ka

   Q: _____   **A:** _____

2. yasumi/iku/desu/rainen/tsumori/ni/ni/natsu/no/dokoka/ka

   Q: _____   **A:** _____

3. nete/asa/no/desu/ashita/mo/made/osoku/ii/ka

Q: _____ **A:** _____

4. dareka/tegami/kakimashita/konshū/ni/o/ka

Q: _____ **A:** _____

5. wa/ashita/desu/yotei/nan/no/ka

Q: _____ **A:** _____

6. iku/itsuka/arimasu/ni/ga/haisha/yotei/ka

Q: _____ **A:** _____

Reading Corner

8. Match the words in _katakana_ to their English translations.

1. memo
2. America
3. yo-yo
4. yard
5. tomato
6. game
7. uniform
8. stamina

a. ヨーヨー
b. ユニホーム
c. ゲーム
d. メモ
e. スタミナ
f. ヤード
g. アメリカ
h. トマト

9. What do these words mean?

1. ムービー _____
2. タイヤ _____
3. ペシミスト _____
4. メキシコ _____
5. ハーモニー _____
6. スマート _____
7. ヨーガ _____
8. ユーモア _____

UNIT 18: I've never done that!

In this unit, you'll practice talking about your experiences and things you have and haven't done, saying how things look, using superlatives, and talking about food and eating.

Match Game

1. Have you ever ...?

Match the sentence halves.

1. Kabuki o	( )	a. tsukatta koto ga arimasu ka.
2. Ōsutoraria no wain o	( )	b. tabeta koto ga arimasu ka.
3. Shinkansen ni	( )	c. sunda koto ga arimasu ka.
4. Chūka ryōri o	( )	d. atta koto ga arimasu ka.
5. Inaka ni	( )	e. mita koto ga arimasu ka.
6. Tai ryōri no resutoran e	( )	f. notta koto ga arimau ka.
7. O-hashi o	( )	g. nonda koto ga arimasu ka.
8. Kenji san no o-kāsan ni	( )	h. itta koto ga arimasu ka.

Talking Point

2. Particles

Mr Ikeda has made it to Sendai in time for the meeting this morning, and is having coffee with Mrs Matsuda while waiting for the meeting to begin. Complete their conversation by filling in the blanks with an appropriate particle. Choose from *ni, wa, ga, to,* or *no.*

Matsuda Ikeda san (1)_____ nemu-sō desu ne.

Ikeda Nemui desu yo. Kesa 5:00 (2)_____ okita kara.

Matsuda Hayai desu ne! Kinō (3)_____ yoru mo dekaketa n' deshō.

Ikeda Ē, Kanadajin no tomodachi (4)_____ issho (5)_____ Tai ryōri (6)_____ resutoran e itta n' desu ga.

Matsuda Tai ryōri desu ka. Watashi (7)_____ tabeta koto (8)_____ nai n' desu ne. Dō deshita ka. Karai deshō.

Ikeda Watashi mo hajimete datta ga, karē raisu (9)_____ suki dakara, Tai no karē (10)_____ shita n' desu ga ...

Matsuda Sore de? Oishikatta?

73

Ikeda	Taihen deshita! Sonna (11)_____ karai mono o ichido mo tabeta koto (12)____ nakatta n' desu yo. Nihon (13)_____ karē raisu yori zutto karai! Ichiban karai karē da to omoimasu. Sūzan san (14)_____ ureshi-sō ni tabeta kedo.
Matsuda	Sùzan san ... sore wa tomodachi (15)_____ namae desu ka. Kanadajin to iimashita ne.
Ikeda	Sō desu. Sūzan Kūpā to iu namae desu. Daigakusei desu.
Matsuda	*(thoughtfully)* Sūzan Kūpā desu ka. Sono namae (16)_____ kiita koto (17)_____ arimasu ne.

Word Power

3. What do you say when ...?

What do you say in the following situations?

1. You are about to begin eating.
2. You and your colleagues are about to have the first drink.
3. The food you are about to eat looks delicious.
4. You have just finished eating.
5. You want the check (bill).
6. The food you have just eaten was delicious.
7. You want to know if your guest would like seconds.
8. You have had enough to eat.

> a. Go-chisō sama deshita.
> b. Mō kekkō desu.
> c. O-naka ga suite iru.
> d. O-kanjō onegai shimasu.
> e. Dō itashimashite.
> f. Oishi-sō!
> g. Kanpai!
> h. Itadakimasu.
> i. O-kawari wa?
> j. Oishikatta!

Language Focus

4. It looks good.

Choose which word or phrase is appropriate to complete these sentences.

1. Ano wanpiisu wa (taka-sō/takai) _____ desu ne. Ikura?
2. Ano eiga wa (omoshiro-sō/omoshiroi) _____ da kedo, jitsu wa sō ja nai n' desu.
3. Kinō no ban, ano atarashii chūka ryōri no resutoran de tabeta kedo, taihen (taka-so datta, takakatta) _____ desu yo.
4. Sūzan san wa (ureshi-sō, ureshii) _____ na kao o shite imasu ne. Dō shite deshō.
5. Kenji san, anata no ōtobai wa (atarashi-sō, atarashii) _____ desu ka.
6. Kore wa (oishi-sō/oishii) _____ desu ne. Itadakimasu!

5. Have you ever...?

The Japanese love to ask foreigners about their Japan experiences. Look at the pictures and write questions like the one in the example. Answer them, too.

Example: Q: Tomaru ryōkan ni tomatta koto ga arimasuka.

A: Hai, arimasu/Iie, arimasen.

1. Q: (noboru) _____

   A: _____

2. Q: (taberu) _____

   A: _____

3. Q: (iku) _____

   A: _____

4. Q: (miru) _____

   A: _____

5. Q: (nomu) _____

   A: _____

6. Q: (kiru) _____

   A: _____

1.

2.

3. KYOTO

4.

5.

6.

6. Which one is best?

Ask questions using the cues provided, like the one in the example. Give your answers, too.

Example: kanji/hiragana/katakana (most difficult?)

Kanji to hiragana to katakana no naka de, dore ga ichiban muzukashii desu ka.

Kanji ga ichiban muzukashii to omoimasu.

1. Japanese curry/Indian curry/Thai curry (hottest?)

   Q: _____

   A: _____

2. Kyoto/Osaka/Nagoya (furthest from Tokyo?)

   Q: _____

   A: _____

3. meat/fish/vegetables (healthiest for you?)

Q: _____

A: _____

4. sake/whiskey/beer (strongest?)

Q: _____

A: _____

5. French food/Japanese food/Chinese food (most expensive?)

Q: _____

A: _____

6. octopus/squid/raw fish (like most?)

Q: _____

A: _____

Reading Corner

7. These are the last of the *katakana* characters. Match them to their *rōmaji* equivalents.

1.	ル	a.	ra
2.	ワ	b.	ri
3.	レ	c.	ru
4.	ラ	d.	re
5.	ン	e.	ro
6.	フ	f.	wa
7.	リ	g.	(w)o
8.	ロ	h.	n

8. Can you identify the following foods and drinks?

1. ワイン _____
2. セロリ _____
3. カリフラワー _____
4. オレンジ _____
5. グレープフルーツ _____

6. マカロニ _____
7. サラダ _____
8. カレーライス _____
9. アイスクリーム _____
10. ベーコン _____

UNIT 19: What happens if you press this?

In this unit, you'll practice conditionals, phrases to use when you visit someone's house, and how to explain the reason for doing something.

Match Game

1. If you get cold ...

Match the sentence halves to find sentences you might hear from someone looking after her overnight guests.

1. Samuku nattara,	( )	a. o-toire wa migi-gawa ni arimasu.
2. Kono suitchi o oshitara,	( )	b. taoru wa kono naka ni arimasu.
3. Neko ga jama dattara,	( )	c. mōfu wa koko ni arimasu.
4. Nemukattara,	( )	d. mado o akete mo ii desu.
5. Kaidan o nobottara,	( )	e. denki ga kiemasu.
6. Atsukattara,	( )	f. daidokoro ni kukkii ga arimasu.
7. O-furo ni hairu n' dattara,	( )	g. soto e dashite kudasai.
8. O-naka ga suitara,	( )	h. dōzo hayaku nete kudasai.

Talking Point

2. Visiting Mrs Mizuno's

After the day's long meeting in Sendai, Mrs Matsuda arrives at her friend Mrs Mizuno's house, where she is staying overnight. Choose the most appropriate words to complete their conversation.

Matsuda Gomen kudasai!

Mizuno Ā, Yoshiko san, (irasshai/o-kaeri nasai) _____ ! Dōzo dōzo, o-hairi kudasai.

Matsuda Arigatō. O-jama (desu/shimasu) _____.

Mizuno Surippa o dōzo. (Nemui/Tsukareta) _____ deshō.

Matsuda Sō desu ne. Totemo nagai ichi-nichi deshita.

Mizuno Ja, dōzo, konban (yukkuri/yasashiku) _____ shite ne. Yoshiko san no heya wa koko desu. Nimotsu o koko ni (okimasu/okurimasu) _____ yo.

Matsuda Kirei-na heya desu ne.

Mizuno Arigatō. Chotto semai (ga/kedo) _____. Mado ga ima aite iru kedo, moshi samuku nattara, mochiron (shimete/akete) _____ mo ii desu yo. Mōfu wa koko ni arimasu. O-furo wa (sō/dō) _____ shimasu ka. Ato de ii desu ka.

Matsuda	Sō desu ne. Ato de ii desu. (Shujin/Go-shujin) _____ wa?
Mizuno	Chotto dekaketa n' desu yo. Biiru o kau tame ni. Sugu (kaeru/kuru) _____ to omou.
Matsuda	Ne, Keiko san, shitsurei desu ga, chotto denwa o tsukatte mo ii? Uchi ni denwa suru tame ni.
Mizuno	Mochiron ii desu yo. Dōzo dōzo.

Word Power

3. At home

Each of the people in these pictures has an appropriate comment among the phrases 1–8 below. Match them up to give them the right thing to say! (Be careful – there are two phrases too many.)

1. O-jama shimasu.

2. Itte 'rasshai.

3. Dō itashimashite.

4. O-kaeri nasai.

5. Dōzo, o-hairi kudasai.

6. Tadaima.

7. Itte kimasu.

8. O-kage sama de.

4. What happens if ...?

Complete these sentences using words from the box. You'll need to change the verbs to the *-tara* form.

1. Kono _____ o _____, dō narimasu ka. Mado ga akimasu.

2. Kono _____ o _____, dō narimasu ka. Denki ga tsukimasu.

3. Kono _____ o _____, dō narimasu ka. Doa ga akimasu.

4. Kono _____ o _____, dō narimasu ka. Enjin ga kakarimasu.

5. Kono _____ o _____, dō narimasu ka. Rajio ga tsukimasu.

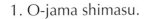

mawasu (x2) osu (x2)
hiku handoru rebā
kagi suitchi botan

Language Focus

5. Why are you going there?

Here's a list of things Mrs Matsuda has to do when she gets back to Tokyo tomorrow. Write sentences explaining what she has to do and why.

Example: yūbinkyoku – kozutsumi o okuru

> Kozutsumi o okuru tame ni, yūbinkyoku
> e ikimasu.

1. _____

2. _____

3. _____

4. _____

5. _____

6. _____

> 1. ginkō – gasu-dai o harau
> 2. Matsudō Depāto – imōto no tanjōbi no purezento o kau
> 3. Honda san ni denwa – raishū no kaigi no koto o sōdan suru
> 4. Supōtsu Sentā – oyogu
> 5. "Poppy" to iu kissaten – Keiko san ni au
> 6. haisha ni denwa – yoyaku o suru

6. Even if it rains ...

Respond to these questions as in the example.

Example: Ame ga futtara, tenisu o yamemasu ka.

> Iie, ame ga futte mo, tenisu o yamemasen yo.

1. Biiru o takusan nondara, futorimasu ka.

   ----

2. Sūtsu wa takakattara, kaimasen ka.

   ----

3. Nagai aida oyoidara, tsukaremasu ne.

   ----

4. Keiko san ga konakattara, tanoshiku nai n' desu ne.

   ----

5. Honda san to sōdan shitara, wakarimasu ne.

   ----

6. Eki made takushii de ittara, densha ni maniaimasu ka.

Reading Corner

7. All of these words have a small *ya, yu, yo,* or vowel combined with the other *katakana* characters. How would you write these words in *rōmaji*, and what do they mean?

1. チェーン・ストア   _____

2. ビューティー・サロン   _____

3. ジュース   _____

4. キャバレー   _____

5. ニュー・ヨーク   _____

6. フェスティバル   _____

7. インタビュー   _____

8. フォーカス   _____

9. ジャーナリスト   _____

10. マティーニ   _____

8. All of these words have a small *tsu*, which doubles the consonant that follows it. Match the beginnings and ends of the words, write the word in *rōmaji*, and then match it to its English meaning, as in the example.

1. ウオ   ッ   チ   _____ ☐

2. ヨーロ   ッ   サージ   _____ ☐

3. スコ   ッ   ト   _____ ☐

4. サ   ッ   ト   _____ ☐

5. マ   ッ   カ   *vokka*   ☐ e

6. メ   ッ   ク   _____ ☐

7. ラケ   ッ   パ   _____ ☐

8. ポケ   ッ   セージ   _____ ☐

9. フ   ッ   カー   _____ ☐

10. クラシ   ッ   トボール   _____ ☐

a. racket	b. message	c. scotch	d. soccer	**e. vodka**
f. football	g. classic, classical	h. Europe	i. massage	j. pocket

UNIT 20: You have to do it!

In this unit, you'll practice describing things you must do, and talking about one event happening before or after another.

Match Game

1. You must do this first!

Match the two parts of each sentence.

1. Taberu mae ni	( )	a.	repōto o kakanakereba narimasen.
2. Pūru ni hairu mae ni	( )	b.	surippā o nuganakereba narimasen.
3. Densha ni noru mae ni	( )	c.	kore mo osanakereba narimasen.
4. Amerika e iku mae ni	( )	d.	ha o migakanakereba narimasen.
5. Kono heya ni hairu mae ni	( )	e.	te o arawanakereba narimasen.
6. Kaigi ga owatte kara	( )	f.	Eigo no benkyō o shinakereba narimasen.
7. Kono botan o oshite kara	( )	g.	shāwā o abinakereba narimasen.
8. Shokuji o shite kara	( )	h.	kippu o kawanakereba narimasen.

Talking Point

2. He's got the job.

Kenji has been offered a job at the American company and will begin working for them in April. He has just told Ms Hayashi about it, before they open the coffee shop for the day. Read through their conversation, and see if the statements which follow are true or false.

Hayashi Omedetō gozaimasu. Itsu hajimaru n' desu ka, sono shigoto wa? Shi-gatsu tsuitachi kara desu ka.

Kenji Hai, sō dakedo, kaisha no shigoto o hajimeru mae ni, iroiro-na kenshū ga aru n' desu yo. San-gatsu tsuitachi kara, shinnyūshain wa kaisha no kenkyū sentā de iroiro-na benkyō o shinakereba naranai n' desu. Chotto kowai yo.

Hayashi Benkyō to iu no wa, donna koto desu ka.

Kenji Eigo ya taipu ya kaisha no rekishi nado, iroiro aru n' desu. Sore kara maiasa hayaku okite, asagohan o taberu mae ni joggingu o shinakereba naranai n' desu.

81

Hayashi   Taihen desu ne. Demo Amerika no kaisha deshō. Dōshite sonna ni kibishii torēningu ga aru n' deshō ka. Mezurashii desu ne.

Kenji   Sō deshō ka.

Hayashi   Ja, ganbatte kudasai ne. Hai, mō jikan desu yo. Yōi wa zenbu dekita n' desu ka. Ja, napukin o tēburu no ue ni oite kara, doa o akete kudasai. Kagi o dōzo.

1. Kenkyū sentā no benkyō ga owatte kara, shigoto wa hajimarimasu.   *True/False*

2. Kenji san dake de wa nakute, kaisha ni hairu hito wa minna kenkyū sentā de kenshū o ukenakereba narimasen.   *True/False*

3. Rekishi no benkyō o shinakereba narimasen.   *True/False*

4. Maiasa asagohan o tabete kara, joggingu ni ikimasu.   *True/False*

5. Hayashi san wa, Amerika no kaisha no kenshū wa futsū kibishiku nai to omoimasu.   *True/False*

6. O-kyakusan wa mada dare mo imasen.   *True/False*

Word Power

3. It depends on ...

Complete the word square using the given verbs in the *-eba* or negative *-nakereba* form as appropriate, to reveal the location of Kenji's new company training center.

aru x 2	yomu	nomu	neru	kuru	atsui	wakaru	suru	ii

1. Kono hon o _ _ _ _ , sugu wakaru to omoimasu.
2. Hoka ni shitsumon ga _ _ _ _ , kore de kaigi o owarimashō.
3. Kono kusuri o _ _ _ _ , sugu genki ni naru to omoimasu.
4. Jikan ga _ _ _ _ , dōzo kite kudasai.
5. _ _ _ _ , mō ichido kiite kudasai.
6. 6:00 made ni _ _ _ _ , watashi wa saki ni ikimasu.
7. Benkyō _ _ _ _ , jōzu ni narimasen yo.
8. _ _ _ _ , mado o akete kudasai.
9. Ashita tenki ga _ _ _ _ , dokoka e ikimashō ka.
10. Sugu _ _ _ _ , ashita okiru koto ga dekinai deshō.

82

Language Focus

4. Rules of the company

Here's part of the list of rules for the training center that Kenji has received from the company. Write sentences about the things he must and must not do, using *-nakereba narimasen* or *-te wa ikemasen*.

Example: Training center rules: – Speak English.

Eigo o hanasanakereba narimasen.

1. _____
2. _____
3. _____
4. _____
5. _____
6. _____

> 1. Go to the classroom by 8:30 each morning.
> 2. Jog before eating breakfast each morning.
> 3. Turn out all lights by 11:30 each night.
> 4. Do not wear shoes in the study center.
> 5. Do not eat in the rooms.
> 6. Do not drink alcohol in the rooms.

5. A typical day at the training center.

The following notes are given to Kenji by a future American colleague to give him an idea of what to expect of a typical day at the company's training center. Help Kenji out by writing proper sentences for him in Japanese. You will need to use the *-te kara* form. The first ones have been done for you.

> 7:00 wake up, get up, go jogging, take shower, eat breakfast, classes begin, classes finish at 4:00, play sports, take bath, eat dinner, watch TV, go to bed

Example: *7:00 ni okimasu. Okite kara, joggingu ni ikimasu. Joggingu ni ...*

_____

_____

_____

_____

Yo-ji ni kurasu ga owarimasu. Kurasu ga owatte kara, supōtsu o shimasu. Supōtsu o

_____

_____

_____

Reading Corner

6. Circle which of the following words is:

1. a country

a.ポスター   b.ポーランド   c.ポケット   d.ポイント

2. furniture

a.テープ   b.テスト   c.テント   d.テーブル

3. a job

a.エンジニア   b.エンジン   c.エプロン   d.エスキモー

4. food

a.オランダ   b.オリンピック   c.オートバイ   d.オムレツ

5. clothing

a.ナプキン   b.ノックアウト   c.ナイトウェア   d.ノルウェー

7. Choose the appropriate word to fill in the blanks.

1.ことしのなつ、＿＿＿＿＿＿＿へいくつもりです。
a.デパート b.ヨーロッパ c.ドイツご d.レストラン

2.えいがのなかで、＿＿＿＿＿＿＿がいちばんすきです。
a.カーネーション b.カーニバル c.アクセサリー d.ミュージカル

3.すみません、＿＿＿＿＿＿＿をください。
a.ブティック b.マタニティー c.ジントニック d.エスカレータ

4.この＿＿＿＿＿＿＿をおせば、どうなりますか。
a.ボタン b.オレンジ c.テレビ d.ベッド

5.あのかいしゃの＿＿＿＿＿＿＿はきびしいですね。
a.カレンダー b.カセット c.トレーニング d.スーツ

UNIT 21: Doing this and that

In this unit, you'll practice describing the time when something happens, talking about a series of activities happening, and describing emotions.

Match Game

1. How did she say it?

Match the sentence halves.

1. "Dō shita n' desu ka. Yonaka no 2:00 desu yo!"
2. "Mō yame nasai!"
3. "O-jisan wa senshū nakunatta,"
4. "Tomodachi wa dare mo inai,"
5. "Eigo de hanashitaku nai – heta da kara,"
6. "Eigo no tesuto de 95-ten totta!"

( ) a. to sabishi-sō ni iimashita.
( ) b. to ureshi-sō ni iimashita.
( ) c. to nemu-sō ni iimashita.
( ) d. to hazukashi-sō ni iimashita.
( ) e. to okori-sō ni iimashita.
( ) f. to kanashi-sō ni iimashita.

Talking Point

2. Home for a vacation

Susan hasn't seen her family for a while, so she's decided to take a trip home to visit everyone. Complete her conversation with Makiko by filling in the gaps with the particles *wa, ga, o, ni,* or *no.*

Makiko Sūzan san (1) _____ inai toki, sabishii yo.

Susan Daijōbu deshō. Makiko san (2) _____ ima sugoku isogashii kara.

Makiko Sonna koto (3) _____ nai wa yo.

Susan *(laughing)* Suru koto (4) _____ ippai aru n' ja nai desu ka. Arubaito (5) _____ shitari, Eigo (6) _____ narattari shite iru deshō? Sore kara atarashii bōifurendo mo iru to kiita kedo.

Makiko Bōifurendo ja nai n' desu yo. Tada no tomodachi desu.

Susan Sore (7) _____ sō kamo shirenai kedo, sono hito kara denwa (8) _____ aru toki, Makiko san (9) _____ itsumo ureshi-sō (10) _____ denwa ni deru ne. Kao mo akaku naru wa yo.

85

Makiko   Mā ... tokorode, ryokō (11) _____ yōi (12) _____ dō desu ka. Zenbu dekimashita ka.

Susan   Iie, mada desu. Kore kara atarashii sūtsukēsu (13) _____ kattari, gasu-dai to denwa-dai (14) _____ harattari, kippu (15) _____ kattari, iroiro shinakereba naranai n' desu yo.

Makiko   E? Hikōki (16) _____ kippu (17) _____ mada katte nai n' desu ka.

Susan   Yoyaku shita kedo, mada haratte inai n' desu.

Word Power

3. Coming and going

Choose two suitable verbs to complete each sentence.

1. Ashita ame ga _____, _____ suru deshō.

2. Sūzan san wa Ikeda san ni _____, _____ shimasu.

3. Hen-na tenki desu ne. _____, _____ shimasu.

4. Shukudai o shite iru toki, jisho o _____, _____ shimasu.

5. Tanaka sensei wa _____, _____ suru kara, chotto mondai desu.

> **konakattari**
> **kumottari**
> **tsukawanakattari**
> **futtari**
> **awanakattari**
> **tsukattari**
> **yandari**
> **kitari**
> **attari**
> **haretari**

Language Focus

4. Doing this and that

Write sentences using the pictures, as in the example.

Example: Kinō nani o shimashita ka.

Uchi de hon o yondari, terebi o mitari shimashita

1. Pātii wa dō deshita ka.

Tanoshikatta desu yo.

2. Haikingu no toki, tenki wa dō deshita ka.

_____

86

3. Nihongo no benkyō wa, dō sureba ii desu ka.

_____ *sureba ii desu.*

4. Gārufurendo wa Igirisujin desu ne. Issho ni hanashite iru toki, nanigo de hanasu n' desu ka.

_____

5. Eiga wa dō deshita ka. Omoshirokatta?

Ē, omoshirokatta yo.

Yoku _____

5. Adjectives and adverbs

Choose which of the alternatives provided is appropriate to complete the sentences.

1. Yuki san wa totemo (jōzu/jōzu-na/jōzu ni) _____ Eigo o hanashimasu ne. Urayamashii!

2. Kinō osoku made biiru o nonde ita kara, kesa totemo (nemui/nemuku) _____ desu yo.

3. Kyō no Eigo no tesuto wa (kantan/kantan-na/kantan ni) _____ dekimashita.

4. (Hayai/Hayaku) _____ yōi o shite kudasai yo. Sugu dekakemasu kara.

5. Sūzan san ga Kanada e kaettara, watashi wa (sabishii/sabishiku) _____ naru to omoimasu yo.

6. When I got home ...

Susan didn't have a particularly good day when she went to buy the new suitcase. Look at the notes she made in her diary, and make sentences like the one in the example about her day, using *toki*.

Example: left home – really good weather

Uchi o deta toki, totemo ii tenki deshita.

1. _____

2. _____

3. _____

4. _____

5. _____

6. _____

(1) went to buy suitcase - met Professor Tanaka.

(2) talking to Professor Tanaka - began to rain!

(3) went into coffee shop - very crowded.

(4) left coffee shop - forgot umbrella!

(5) got onto train home - head began to hurt.

(6) got home - very tired!

Reading Corner

7. Match up the numbers with their equivalents in *kanji*.

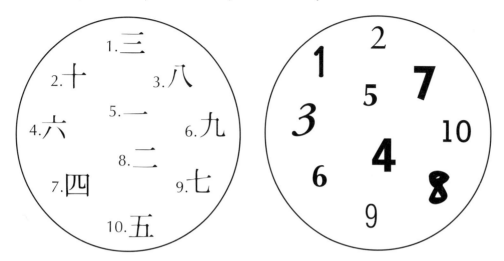

8. Read the sentences describing Susan's afternoon in the department store, and mark on the store plan what she bought or did on each floor.

1. 六かいでちいさいタオルを二まいかいました。

2. 四かいでなにもかいませんでした。

3. 五かいでやすいボールペンを六ぽんかいました。

4. 二じに八かいのきっさてんでコーヒーをのみました。

5. 二かいであかいスーツケースをかいました。

6. ちか一かいでカメラのフィルムを四ほんかいました。

8	
7	
6	
5	
4	
3	
2	
1	
B1	
B2	
B3	

UNIT 22: Celebrations!

In this unit, you'll practice talking about giving and receiving things, times of celebration throughout the year, and how to express doing two things at the same time.

Match Game

1. Same meaning

Match the sentences which have a similar meaning.

1. Nagai aida atte imasen.
2. Taishita byōki ja arimasen.
3. 12-gatsu desu.
4. Kore wa, katta mono ja arimasen.
5. Tanaka san ni sore o agemashita.

( )   a. Sorosoro bōnenkai no toki desu.
( )   b. Kare wa sore o moraimashita.
( )   c. Daijōbu desu.
( )   d. Hisashiburi desu.
( )   e. Kore o moraimashita.

Talking Point

2. Visiting the hospital

On his way home from work, Mr Matsuda is going to visit his boss, who is in the hospital. While waiting on the train platform he sees an acquaintance, Ms Saitō. Choose which of the words given in parentheses is most appropriate to complete their conversation.

Matsuda   Saitō san ja arimasen ka.

Saitō   Ara, Matsuda san, dōmo. (O-hisashiburi/O-genki) _ _ _ _ _ _ _ _ desu ne.

Matsuda   Sō desu ne. Mina san (daijōbu/o-genki) _ _ _ _ _ _ _ _ desu ka.

Saitō   Hai, o-kage sama de. *(noticing the flowers he is carrying)* O-hana kirei desu ne. Dareka ni (moratta/ageta) _ _ _ _ _ _ _ _ n' desu ka.

Matsuda   Iie, chigaimasu yo.

Saitō   Ā, wakarimashita. Okusan ni (itadaku/ageru) _ _ _ _ _ _ _ n' desu ne. O-tanjōbi desu ka.

Matsuda   Chigaimasu! Tada, uchi no kaisha no buchō ga chotto byōki de, byōin ni (ireta/haitta) _ _ _ _ _ kara, watashi wa kore kara (o-mimai/mi) _ _ _ _ _ ni iku n' desu.

Saitō   Sō desu ka. Daijōbu desu ka.

Matsuda   Hai hai, (dō shita/taishita) _ _ _ _ _ _ _ byōki ja nai n' desu. (Jitsu wa/Tokorode) _ _ _ _ _ _ _, jibun no uchi yori byōin no hō ga ii to buchō wa itte imashita yo. Shizuka da shi, beddo de (nenagara/inagara) _ _ _ _ _ _ _ terebi o miru koto ga dekiru shi, shokuji o shinagara shimbun o yomu koto mo dekiru kara!

Saitō   Mā, sore wa sō desu ne.

Word Power

3. Celebrations

Look at the clues, and then find the names of the 10 days of celebration and/or present-giving in the word square.

1. New Year
2. birthday
3. wedding
4. Christmas
5. Valentine's Day
6. graduation
7. summer gift-giving season in Japan
8. winter gift-giving season in Japan
9. year-end party
10. visiting someone in hospital

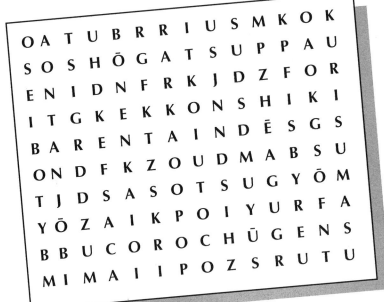

4. Giving and taking

Choose which of the following verbs is most appropriate in each case to complete the sentences: *morau, itadaku, yaru, ageru, sashiageru.*

1. Nichiyōbi wa okāsan no tanjōbi desu ne. Nani o _ _ _ _ _ _ _ mashō ka.

2. Sorosoro o-chūgen no toki desu ne. Kaisha no shachō san ni nani o _ _ _ _ _ _ _ mashō ka.

3. Kono hana wa kirei desu ne! O-mimai ni Matsuda san kara _ _ _ _ _ _ _ mashita.

4. Kesa Tanaka sensei ni hagaki o _ _ _ _ _ _ _ mashita yo. Hawai kara!

5. Kenji san, neko ni miruku o _ _ _ _ _ _ _ te kudasai.

Language Focus

5. Don't do this while you're doing that!

One of the reasons Mr Matsuda's boss is enjoying his stay in the hospital is that he can get away from all his wife's strict rules for him and his children. Write sentences about her rules using the cues, as in the example.

Example: No talking while eating!

Mono o tabenagara, hanasu no wa dame desu.

1. No watching TV while studying!

2. No reading the paper while having a meal!

3. No eating while talking on the phone!

4. No drinking coffee while using the computer!

5. No eating in bed!

6. No listening to a Walkman while doing homework!

6. Making conversation

Find the two conversations which have been mixed up below.

A1. Matsuda san, omoshiroi nekutai desu ne.

A2. Kirei-na kaban o katta n' desu ne.

B1. Ē, purezento desu. Ashita wa kanai no tanjōbi da kara.

B2. Ē, jitsu wa amari suki ja nai kedo, musume ni moratta kara ...

A1. Sō desu ka. Okusan ni ageru n' desu ka. Ii iro desu ne.

A2. Moratta n' desu ka. Wakarimashita. Iro wa chotto ...

B1. Sō desu ne – burū to pinku! Demo musume wa kono iro ga suki da to itta kara ...

B2. Ē, kanai wa burū ga suki da kara.

A1. Nan-sai ni narimasu ka.

A2. Nan-sai desu ka.

B1. 8-sai desu.

B2. 32-sai.

Reading Corner

7. Match the words on the left with their equivalents on the right.

1. Christmas	a. おしょうがつ
2. birthday	b. おせいぼ
3. new year	c. クリスマス
4. wedding	d. バレンタイン・ディ
5. graduation	e. ぼうねんかい
6. winter gift-giving season	f. たんじょうび
7. year-end party	g. そつぎょう
8. Valentine's Day	h. けっこんしき

8. Mr Tanaka received various presents this year. Write down in the boxes what he received, when, and from whom.

1. たなかさんはたんじょうび にはやしさんから スカーフをもらいました。

2. バレンタイン・ディにもりたさんがたなかさん にチョコレートをあげました。

3. けっこんしたとき、やまぐちせんせいからとけい をいた だきました。

4. クリスマスにたなかさんは おかあさんからセーター をもらいました。

WHAT	WHEN	FROM WHOM

UNIT 23: Shall I do it for you?

In this unit, you'll practice ways to express doing things for other people, and talking about things you are thinking of doing. There is also more practice on giving and receiving.

Match Game

1. Doing things for people

Match each person with the sentence or request they are most likely to hear.

1. isha	( )	a. Mō sukoshi mijikaku kitte kudasai.
2. sensei	( )	b. Terebi o naoshite moraitai n' desu ga.
3. untenshu	( )	c. Biiru 20-pon, uchi e todokete moraemasu ka.
4. hisho	( )	d. Nodo o mite itadakemasu ka.
5. toko-ya	( )	e. Koko de tomete kuremasu ka.
6. denki-ya	( )	f. Kono repōto ni sain o shite itadakemasu ka.
7. saka-ya	( )	g. Kono kotoba no imi o oshiete itadakemasu ka.
8. shachō	( )	h. Kono fakkusu o Ōsaka shisha ni okutte kureru?

Talking Point

2. She cut my hair for me.

Kenji has just arrived for his part-time job at the coffee shop, and Ms Hayashi is amused to see he has a very peculiar haircut. Put their lines in the correct order to find out what happened.

Hayashi Matsuda san, atama, dō shita n' desu ka.

1. **Hayashi** Ā, sō desu ne. Arubaito no kyūryō-bi wa raishū desu ne.

2. **Kenji** Sō desu ne. Dō shimashō? Konban daigaku no pātii ga aru kedo, mō hazukashikute, ikitaku nai n' desu yo. Yameyō to omotte imasu.

3. **Hayashi** O-kāsan ga? Dō shite toko-ya ni ikanakatta n' desu ka.

4. **Hayashi** *(laughing)* Sō desu ka. Dakara o-kāsan ni kitte moratta n' desu ka. Demo, chotto mijikai desu ne.

5. **Kenji** Jitsu wa, toko-ya ni ikō to omotte ita kedo, o-kane ga nakute ...

6. **Hayashi** Sore wa zannen desu ne. Kyō arubaito ga owatte kara, toko-ya ni ittara dō desu ka.

7. **Kenji**   *(embarrassed)* Kami no ke desu ka. Chotto nagakatta no de, haha ga kitte kureta n' desu ga.

8. **Kenji**   Ikitai kedo, o-kane ga ...

Kenji   Hayashi san, warui kedo, raishū no kawari ni, kyō haratte itadakeru deshō ka.

Word Power

3. Odd man out

Circle the word which doesn't fit in each of the groups below.

1.   tokoya   sakaya   taiya   yaoya   panya

2.   kyūryō   kyūkō   o-kane   en   o-tsuri

3.   jisho   zasshi   kyōkasho   shōsetsu   kotoba

4.   kawaii   zannen   kawaisō   hidoi   kurushii

5.   ikō   ittara   iimasu   itte   ikitai

4. More giving and receiving

It's the end of term, and everyone is giving presents. Complete Susan's sentences about the presents she's given and received, using the lists below. Use *kureru*, *kudasaru*, *ageru*, or *sashiageru*, as in the example.

   Example: Wada sensei ga watashi ni jisho o

   Kudasaimashita.
   ----

1. Chichi to haha ga kaban o

   ----

2. Makiko san ni Eigo no hon o

   ----

3. Wada sensei ni e o

   ----

4. Makiko san no o-kāsan ga hana o

   ----

5. Makiko san ga nekkuresu o

   ----

6. Tomoko san ni saifu o

RECEIVED:
Prof. Wada - dictionary
mum and dad - briefcase
Makiko - necklace
Makiko's mother - flowers

GAVE:
Makiko - English book
Tomoko - purse
Prof. Wada - picture
(from all of us!)

Language Focus

5. I'm thinking about doing that.

Susan will be starting her new job when she gets back from Canada, and she intends to make a new start in other areas of her life, too. Using the cues, write sentences about her ideas like the one in the example.

Example: (Look for a new apartment?)   *Atarashii apāto o sagasō to omotte imasu.*

1. (Go to Australia next summer?)

2. (Have my hair cut short?)

3. (Study Spanish?)

4. (Give up chocolate?)

5. (Buy a new car?)

6. Word order

Rearrange the words to make sentences or questions.

1. ga/yomu koto/oshiete/kono/kudasai/o/kara/ji/dekinai

   Hai, sono ji wa "higashi" to yomimasu.

2. atarashii/imasu/Honda/wa/san/omotte/apāto/sagasō/o/to

   Sō desu ka. Doko de?

3. to/no/wa/yameyō/shigoto/ja nai/imasu/ima/suki/kara/kangaete

   ----

   Demo yametara, sono ato dō shimasu ka.

7. Do me a favor!

Look at the pictures and decide which of the sentences is being said by the person shown in each one.

1. a. Mō sukoshi mijikaku kitte moraitai n' desu ga.
   b. Mō sukoshi mijikaku shite agemashō ka.

2. a. Eiga o mi ni ikitai kedo, o-kane ga nai kara, kashite kureru?
   b. Eiga o mi ni itte moraitai kedo, o-kane ga nai kara, kashite ageru?

3. a. Ii kuruma deshō. Chichi ni kashite moraimashita.
   b. Ii kuruma deshō. Chichi ga kashite agemashita.

4. a. Kono shashin wa, ani ni totte agemasu.

   b. Kono shashin wa, ani ga totte kureta n' desu.

5. a. Ashita wa tanjōbi dakara, kanai ni kēki o tsukutte kuremasu.

   b. Ashita wa kanai no tanjōbi dakara, kēki o tsukutte agemasu.

Reading Corner

8. Match the *kanji* to the appropriate pronunciation.

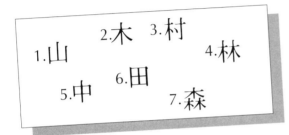

1.山　2.木　3.村　4.林　5.中　6.田　7.森

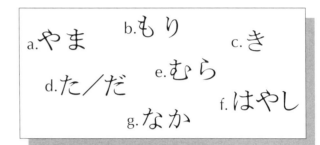

a.やま　b.もり　c.き　d.た／だ　e.むら　f.はやし　g.なか

9. Rewrite the following sentences in *rōmaji*.

1. 林さんは森田さんになにをあげましたか。

   _____

2. 村田さんと山田さんはけっこんするときききましたが。ほんとう？

   _____

3. 田中さんも木村さんもパーティーにきてくれました。

   _____

4. すみませんが、これを森さんと山中さんにおくってください。

   _____

UNIT 24: Review

1. Matching

Match the questions to the answers.

1. Itsu?		
2. Doko?	( )	a. Sensei.
3. Dō shite?	( )	b. 5-sai.
4. Dare?	( )	c. Ano atarashii no.
5. Nani de?	( )	d. Basu de.
6. Ikutsu?	( )	e. Kinō.
7. Nani?	( )	f. Depāto de.
8. Dore?	( )	g. Suki da kara.
	( )	h. Hon.

2. Set phrases

What do you say in the following situations?

1. Kore kara tabe-hajimeru toki, nan to iimasu ka.

----

2. Nanika o moratta toki, nan to iimasu ka.

----

3. Nagai aida atte inai hito ni atta toki, nan to iimasu ka.

----

4. Denwa ni deta toki, nan to iimasu ka.

----

5. Kissaten ya resutoran ni haitta toki, uētoresu wa nan to iimasu ka.

----

6. Uchi o deru toki, nan to iimasu ka.

----

7. Dareka ga "Arigatō" to ittara, nan to iimasu ka.

----

8. Tomodachi no tanjōbi ni nan to iimasu ka.

----

3. Crossword

Find the missing words from the sentences below to complete the crossword.

ACROSS:

1. _ _ _ _ _ deshō. Konban hayaku neta hō ga ii desu yo.

6. _ _ _ _ _ fuyu sukii ni ikimasu.

8. Kyō wa futsuka ja nai n' desu yo. _ _ _ _ _ desu.

9. Nihon no uta o _ _ _ _ _ koto ga arimasu ka.

12. _ _ _ _ _ ga futtara, samuku narimasu yo!

15. Makiko san no o-niisan ni _ _ _ _ _ koto ga arimasu ka? Ii hito desu yo!

16. Kare wa totemo _ _ _ _ _ kao o shimashita kara, kowakatta desu.

17. _ _ _ _ _ ga areba, tabako o yameta hō ga ii desu.

18. Hazukashii kara, kao mo _ _ _ _ _ mo akaku narimashita.

19. 10:00 ni _ _ _ _ _ ni tsuitara, densha ni maniau to omoimasu.

20. Watashi no uchi e _ _ _ _ _ dō desu ka.

23. Ano hoteru no heya wa kirei da kedo, chotto _ _ _ _ _ desu.

25. Mokuyōbi wa isogashii kedo, kayōbi wa _ _ _ _ _ imasu.

26. Fuyu to aki to, dochira no hō ga ame ga _ _ _ _ _ desu ka.

27. Ashita ame ga _ _ _ _ _ to kiita kedo, haikingu wa dō shimasu ka.

DOWN:

1. Watashi wa maiasa kono kusuri o _ _ _ _ _ naranai to isha ga iimashita.

2. Maishū getsuyōbi to _ _ _ _ _ ni pūru de oyogimasu.

3. Kesa no densha wa taihen konde ita kedo, _ _ _ _ _ suite imasu ne.

4. Kanai wa _ _ _ _ _ ga dai-suki da kedo, watashi wa sakana no hō ga suki desu.

5. Takahashi san wa kaigi ni _ _ _ _ _ kedo, Saitō san wa demasen deshita.

7. Kore wa oishi-sō desu ne. _ _ _ _ _ !

10. Sakana _ _ _ _ _ niku to, dochira no hō ga suki desu ka.

11. Eki no mae ni _ _ _ _ _ iru hito wa dare desu ka.

13. Tomoko chan, osoi desu yo. Denki o _ _ _ _ _ kudasai.

14. Kami o kite moratta deshō. Chotto _ _ _ _ _ ja nai?

21. Kore o tabete mo _ _ _ _ _ desu ka.

22. Tōkyō de dareka ni au yotei ga _ _ _ _ _ to iimashita.

23. _ _ _ _ _ ga takakute, futotte iru hito desu.

24. Chotto wakaranakatta kara, _ _ _ _ _ ichido setsumei shite kudasai.

4. A, B, or C?

Choose the most appropriate answer to each question.

1. Tanjōbi ni nani o moratta n' desu ka.

   a. Chichi ga tokei o kuremashita.

   b. Kaban o ageta n' desu.

   c. Haha ga hana o moratta n' desu.

2. Moshi yokattara, dōzo kore o tsukatte kudasai.

   a. Hai, ii desu.

   b. Yokatta!

   c. Dōmo arigatō.

3. Wada san no hō ga se ga takai desu ka.

   a. Hai, Wada san yori.

   b. Hai, sō desu.

   c. Wada san no hō ga se ga hikui desu.

4. Yōka ka kokonoka wa ikaga desu ka.

   a. Iie, aite imasen.

   b. Yōka mo kokonoka mo daijōbu desu.

   c. Yōka no hō ga warui desu.

5. Kaze o hiita toki, nani o shitara ii desu ka.

   a. Kusuri o nondara ii desu.

   b. Sō shitara ii desu.

   c. Kaze o hikanaide kudasai.

5. Grandma's birthday

Who's who in the family photo? Read the description below, label each person, and draw in the four objects which are missing.

Kore wa uchi no niwa de totta shashin desu. Kono hi wa obāsan no tanjōbi datta kara, obāsan wa ichiban mae ni suwatte imasu. Kirei-na hana o motte imasu. O-bāsan no tonari ni imōto no Tomoko ga tatte imasu. Hen-na bōshi o kabutte imasu ne! Ichiban se ga takai hito wa ushiro ni tatte imasu. Kare wa tonari no ie no Wada san desu. Kami no mijikai otoko no ko wa Wada san no musuko no Jun chan desu. Jun chan to Wada san no aida ni tatte iru hito wa chichi de, chichi no mae de megane o kakete, suwatte iru hito wa haha desu. Ichiban hidari no chotto futotte iru hito wa watashi desu. Obāsan ni ageru purezento o motte imasu.

1. _____

2. _____

3. _____

4. _____

5. _____

6. _____

7. _____

6. All about you

Answer these questions about yourself.

1. Ima nani o kite imasu ka. _____

2. Kyō no tenki wa dō desu ka. _____

3. Kodomo no toki, doko ni sunde imashita ka. _____

4. Itsu kara Nihongo o benkyō shite imasu ka. _____

5. Atama ga itai toki nani o shimasu ka. _____

6. Megane o kakete imasu ka. _____

7. Anata no tanjōbi wa itsu desu ka. _____

8. Tai ryōri no resutoran de tabeta koto ga arimasu ka. _____

7. Do you know ...?

Match the general knowledge questions to the correct answers.

1. にほんで一ばんたかい山は
   なんですか。

a. オーストラリア
   にいます。

2. イタリアのおかねはなんと
   いいますか。

b. ポルトガルごで
   はなします。

3. ブラジルではなにごではな
   しますか。

c. メトロです。

4. カンガルーはどこのくにに
   いますか。

d. リラです。

5. パリのちかてつはなんとい
   いますか。

e. ふじさんです。

REFERENCE
SECTION

Answer Key

Unit 1

1. 1. f 2. e 3. d 4. a 5. c 6. b

2. Hai, kara, no, Watashi, namae, Sumimasen

3. 1. 0492-32-1131 2. 03-3231-4253 3. 0726-81-3828
   4. 0988-62-7964 5. 078-221-6437

4. 1. Matsuda san wa gakusei desu ka. 2. Sensei no meishi
   desu. 3. Tanaka san wa Tōkyō kara desu. 4. Denwa bangō
   wa 4163-7709 desu. 5. Namae wa nan desu ka. 6. Sensei wa
   Furansujin desu ka.

5. 1. Igirisu no kuruma desu. 2. Amerika no konpyūtā desu.
   3. Furansu no wain desu. 4. Itaria no kaban desu. 5. Nihon
   no terebi desu.

6. 1. Maeda san no meishi desu ka. Iie, chigaimasu. Matsuda
   san no meishi desu. 2. Eigo no hon desu ka. Hai, sō desu.
   3. Igirisu no kuruma desu ka. Hai, sō desu. 4. Kanadajin
   desu ka. Iie, chigaimasu. Amerikajin desu. 5. Ogawa san no
   denwa bangō desu ka. Hai, sō desu.

7. 1. i 2. a 3. u 4. o 5. e

8. 1. ue (over, above) 2. iie (no) 3. ai (love) 4. aoi (blue-green)
   5. ie (house)

Unit 2

1. 1. c 2. e 3. b 4. a 5. d

2. 9-3-6-4-8-1-5-2-7

3. Drinks-biiru, wain, o-cha, kōhii Languages-Nihongo, Eigo,
   Furansugo, Supeingo People-sensei, Amerikajin, gakusei,
   tomodachi Electrical goods-konpyūtā, bideo, terebi, rajio

4. 1. 12:30 2. 1:30 3. 8:00 4. 10:30 5. 2:00 6. 4:30

5. 1. Arubaito wa nan-ji kara desu ka. 2. (Arubaito wa) Nan-ji
   made desu ka. 3. Kissaten no namae wa nan desu ka.
   4. Denwa bangō wa nan desu ka.

6. 1. Furansujin ja arimasen. 2. Amerika kara ja arimasen.
   3. Kōhii ja arimasen. 4. Doitsu no kuruma ja arimasen.
   5. Matsuda san no hon ja arimasen.

7. 1. (name) desu. 2. Hai, sō desu. OR Iie, (Amerikajin) desu.
   3. (Rondon) kara desu. 4. Hai, sō desu. OR Iie, (sensei) desu.

8. 1. gi 2. ka 3. gu 4. ke 5. ko 6. ge 7. ku 8. ga 9. ki 10. go

9. 1. b 2. d 3. c 4. d 5. a 6. b

Unit 3

1. 1. c 2. a 3. b 4. e 5. f 6. d

2. wa, ni, no, wa, no, no, ni, wa, ni

3. Across: pantsu, burausu, sētā, kōto, nekutai, sūtsu
   Down: sukāto, pajama, doresu, jaketto

4. 1. kyū, go, yon 2. dono, kono 3. rajio, eiga, bideo 4. jūsu,
   kōcha, biiru 5. shatsu, pantsu, kutsu 6. dōzo, dōmo arigatō

5. B1. chika ikkai 1F. ikkai 2F. nikai 3F. sankai 4F. yonkai
   5F. gokai 6F. rokkai 7F. nanakai 1. Kissaten wa nankai ni
   arimasu ka. Chika ikkai ni arimasu. 2. Kaban to handobaggu
   wa nankai ni arimasu ka. Ikkai ni arimasu. 3. Sukāto wa
   nankai ni arimasu ka. Nikai ni arimasu. 4. Tokei to kamera
   wa nankai ni arimasu ka. Rokkai ni arimasu. 5. Resutoran wa
   nankai ni arimasu ka. Nanakai ni arimasu.

6. (checks) 3, 5, 7, 8 (crosses) 1, 2, 4, 6, 9

7. 1. sa 2. ze 3. shi 4. za 5. so 6. zu 7. se 8. zo 9. su 10. ji

8. 1. isu (chair) 2. kasa (umbrella) 3. chiisai (small) 4. gakusei
   (student) 5. asoko (over there) 6. shizuka (quiet) 7. eki
   (station) 8. ōkii (big)

Unit 4

1. 1. f 2. g 3. b 4. d 5. e 6. a 7. c

2. kono, koko, kudasai, shitsurei, daigaku, o-genki, konban,
   arimasen

3. 1. 5:50 2. 10:15 3. 1:20 4. 3:45 5. 8:05

4. 1. Eiga wa ni-ji jip-pun kara san-ji go-jip-pun made desu.
   2. Kissaten wa hachi-ji kara roku-ji han made desu. 3. Eigo
   no kurasu wa san-ji jū-go-fun kara go-ji jū-go-fun made
   desu. 4. Depāto wa hachi-ji kara roku-ji han made desu.
   5. Resutoran wa roku-ji han kara jū-ichi-ji yon-jū-go-fun
   made desu.

5. books and magazines under the bed, motorcycle tire
   between the bed and the desk, tennis racket and ball next to
   the tire, cassette tapes and CDs on the desk, coat and
   pyjamas behind the door, dog on the bed

6. (checks) 1. a 2. a 3. b 4. b 5. a

7. 1. de 2. chi 3. to 4. zu 5. ta 6. tsu 7. te 8. da 9. ji
   10. do

8. 1. d 2. f 3. h 4. k 5. b 6. l 7. j 8. a 9. e 10. i 11. c
   12. g

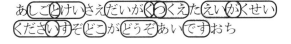

Unit 5

1. 1. d 2. g 3. a 4. f 5. c 6. b 7. h 8. e

2. nomimasen, arimasen, kaerimasu, desu, desu, tsukurimasu,
   tsukurimasen, shimasu, ikimasu, wakarimasen, desu,
   ikimasu

3. Free answers

103

4. 1. Matsuda san wa itsumo nan-ji ni okimasu ka.
   2. Kanojo wa donna shigoto o shimasu ka.
   3. Matsuda san wa sono shigoto ga suki desu ka.
   4. Konban doko no resutoran e ikimasu ka.
   5. Dare ga itsumo asagohan o tsukurimasu ka.

5. 1. d 2. e 3. a 4. f 5. b 6. c

6. 1. Matsuda san wa bōringu ga suki desu ka. Hai, suki desu.
   2. Kenji san wa aisu sukēto ga suki desu ka. Iie, amari suki ja
   arimasen. 3. Tomoko chan wa kabuki ga suki desu ka. Iie,
   dai-kirai desu. 4. Matsuda san wa aisu sukēto ga suki desu
   ka. Iie, kirai desu. 5. Matsuda san to Kenji san wa eiga ga
   suki desu ka. Hai, dai-suki desu.

7. na-5 ni-2 nu-7 ne-10 no-12

8. 1. g 2. b 3. f 4. e 5. c 6. a 7. i 8. h 9. d 10. k

Unit 6

1. 1. f 2. d 3. e 4. g 5. a 6. h 7. c 8. b

2. 5-1-6-4-2-3

3. My family: haha-f, chichi-m, ane-f, ani-m, imōto-f, otōto-m,
   kanai-f, shujin-m. Your family: okāsan-f, otōsan-m, onēsan-f,
   oniisan-m, imōtosan-f, otōtosan-m, okusan-f, go-shujin-m

4. 1. Kenji san no okāsan wa yon-jū-nana-sai desu. 2. (Kenji san
   no) otōsan wa yon-jū-has-sai desu. 3. (Kenji san no)
   imōtosan wa jū-yon-sai desu. 4. (Kenji san no) o-nēsan wa
   ni-jū-go-sai desu. 5. (Kenji san no) o-nēsan no go-shujin wa
   ni-jū-roku-sai desu.

5. Free answers

6. 1. supōtsu sentā de tenisu o shimasu. 2. resutoran de
   hirugohan o tabemasu. 3. depāto de kaimono o shimasu.
   4. kissaten de kōhii o nomimasu. 5. uchi de bangohan o
   tsukurimasu.

7. (clockwise from top) fu, pi, ho, pu, bi, he, ha, ba, po, be,
   bu, bo

8. 1. b 2. c 3. b 4. a 5. c 6. a

Unit 7

1. 1. g 2. d 3. a 4. i 5. h 6. e 7. b 8. c 9. f

2. 1. F 2. F 3. F 4. T 5. T 6. T

3. akai, kuroi, shiroi, kiiro, aoi, chairo, burū, guriin, pinku,
   orenji, murasaki, midori

4. 1. 2,300 2. 23,000 3. 30,550 4. 310 5. 8,830 6. 1,300
   7. 105,000 8. 15,600

5. 1. Handobaggu wa ni-man is-sen en deshita. 2. Sētā wa ichi-
   man yon-sen san-byaku en deshita. 3. Sukāfu wa roku-sen
   yon-hyaku en deshita. 4. Tokei wa nana-sen go-hyaku en
   deshita. 5. Zasshi wa kyū-hyaku yon-jū en deshita.
   6. Sukāto wa ni-man ni-sen kyū-hyaku en deshita.

6. 1. Kono akai sukāfu wa dare no desu ka. 2. Kenji san no
   arubaito wa muzukashii desu ka. 3. Matsuda san wa
   kaimono ga suki desu ka. 4. Kissaten no ongaku wa urusai
   desu ka. 5. Matsuda san no atarashii kutsu wa ikura deshita
   ka. 6. Ano atarashii resutoran wa oishii desu ka.

7. 1. f 2. h 3. a 4. g 5. c 6. i 7. b 8. d 9. e

8.

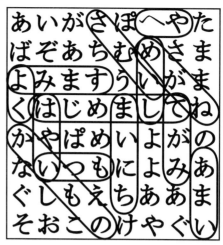

Unit 8

1. 1. d 2. f 3. g 4. h 5. c 6. a 7. b 8. e

2. shimashita, narimashita, ikimashita, deshita, deshita,
   tabemashita, deshita, nomimashita, nomimasen deshita, ja
   arimasen deshita, kaimashita, ikimashita, narimashita,
   kaerimashita

3. 1. nichiyōbi 2. mokuyōbi 3. kayōbi 4. suiyōbi 5. getsuyōbi
   6. doyōbi 7. kinyōbi

4. 1. (Magome eki kara) Haneda kūkō made densha de
   ikimashita. 2. (Haneda kūkō kara) Ōsaka kūkō made hikōki
   de ikimashita. 3. (Ōsaka kūkō kara) Ōsaka eki made basu de
   ikimashita. 4. (Ōsaka eki kara) Machida eki made chikatetsu
   de ikimashita. 5. (Machida eki kara) uchi made takushii de
   ikimashita.

5. 1. Kayōbi no gogo, nani o shimashita ka. Kaigi o shimashita.
   2. Kayōbi no yoru, nani o shimashita ka. Tōkyō e
   kaerimashita. 3. Suiyōbi no asa, nani o shimashita ka. Ōsaka
   shutchō no repōto o kakimashita. 4. Mokuyōbi no asa, nani
   o shimashita ka. O-kāsan ni denwa shimashita.
   5. Kinyōbi no yoru, nani o shimashita ka. Wada san to (issho
   ni) bangohan o tabemashita.

6. 1. O-kāsan ni tegami o kakimasen deshita. 2. Ōsaka Hoteru
   ni denwa shimashita. 3. Ōsaka shisha no sērusu repōto o
   yomimasen deshita. 4. Kuroi sūtsu o kaimashita. 5. Ōsaka no
   o-kyakusan to hanashimasen deshita.

7. 1. doko 2. nan-ji 3. doko 4. nani 5. nani 6. dare

8. 1. c 2. g 3. e 4. a 5. h 6. f 7. b 8. d

9. 1. e denwa o shimasu 2. a omoshiroi 3. g hiru-gohan
   4. i wakarimashita 5. j shitsurei shimasu 6. b atarashii
   7. c arigatō 8. h warui 9. f ikura 10. d ushiro

Unit 9

1. 1. 1997 2. 1960 3. 1983 4. 1779 5. 1893 6. 1946
   7. 1992 8. 1979

2. 1. F 2. T 3. T 4. F 5. T 6. T

3. 1. atsui 2. konbanwa 3. otōto 4. hidari 5. tanoshikatta
   6. kaerimashita

4. 5-9-2-6-1-3-7-8-4

5. 1. (Sen kyū-hyaku) hachi-jū-ni-nen kara (Sen kyū-hyaku) hachi-jū-go-nen made Igirisu ni sunde imashita. (kazoku to issho ni). 2. Daigaku de keizai o benkyō shimashita. 3. Supeingo mo benkyō shimashita. 4. (Sen kyū-hyaku) kyū-jū-ni-nen kara (sen kyū-hyaku) kyū-jū-san-nen made Supein de Eigo o oshiemashita. 5. (Sen kyū-hyaku) kyū-jū-san-nen ni Nihon e/ni kimashita.

6. 1. Kodomo no toki, me ga warukatta (desu) ga, ima wa daijōbu desu. 2. Kodomo no toki, Rondon ni sunde imashita ga, ima wa Pari ni sunde imasu. 3. Kodomo no toki, chiizu ga suki ja nakatta (desu) ga/suki ja arimasen deshita ga, ima wa dai-suki desu. 4. Kodomo no toki, supōtsu o yoku shimashita ga, ima wa zenzen shimasen. 5. Kodomo no toki, terebi wa omoshirokatta (desu) ga, ima wa zenzen omoshiroku arimasen. 6. Kodomo no toki, fuyu wa samukatta (desu) ga, ima wa amari samuku arimasen.

7. 1. ryōri 2. kaisha 3. kyonen 4. senshū 5. hyaku 6. byōki 7. chairo 8. jōzu 9. o-kyakusan 10. shumi

8. 1. chotto-a little 2. gakkō-school 3. issho-together 4. irasshaimase-welcome 5. ikkai-first floor 6. kissaten-coffee shop 7. shutchō-business trip 8. zasshi-magazine 9. roppyaku-six hundred 10. atsukatta-was hot

Unit 10

1. 1. d 2. f 3. e 4. h 5. g 6. a 7. b 8. c

2. 3-7-9-5-1-8-2-4

3. 2. department store 3. restaurants 4. movie theater 6. bank 7. coffee shop 8. post office

4. 1. Tsugi no kado de hidari ni magatte kudasai. 2. Yukkuri hanashite kudasai. 3. Massugu itte kudasai. 4. Mado o shimete kudasai. 5. Mō ichido itte kudasai. 6. Sono shiroi tatemono no mae de tomete kudasai.

5. 1. Iie, kyō denwa shite kudasai. 2. Iie, takushii de itte kudasai. 3. Iie, futatsu katte kudasai. 4. Iie, Ishii san ni kiite kudasai. 5. Iie, Eigo de hanashite kudasai. 6. Iie, ato de tsukutte kudasai.

6. 1. c (atama) 2. b (kuroi) 3. d (ane) 4. a (chikatetsu) 5. c (ginkō)

7. 1. b 2. d 3. a 4. b 5. d

Unit 11

1. 1. f, g 2. b, h 3. a, d 4. c, e

2. motte imasu, motte imasu, ikimashō, tatte imasu, tatte imasu, kabutte imasu, motte imasu, matte imasu, matte imasu, shimashō, demashō, shimashō

3. 1. Akai bōshi o kabutte imasu. 2. Kuroi T-shatsu o kite imasu. 3. Shiroi shatsu o kite imasu. 4. Kuroi zubon o haite imasu. 5. Shiroi suniikā o haite imasu. 6. Guriin no kaban o motte imasu.

4. 1. sukāto, kutsu, kutsushita, zubon, sūtsu, nekutai 2. resutoran, konsāto, kissaten, eiga, gekijō 3. sofā, tēburu, terebi, isu, tsukue 4. tenisu, gorufu, suiei, sukii, haikingu, sakkā 5. yūbinkyoku, ginkō, gakkō, depāto, eigakan, toshokan

5. 1. Doko de aimashō ka. 2. Nan-ji ni ikimashō ka. 3. Nani o kimashō ka. 4. Nani o motte ikimashō ka. 5. Densha de ikimashō ka.

6. 1. Ashita nan-ji ni eki de aimashō ka. 2. Sūzan san wa kuroi sukāto o haite imasu ka. 3. Ame ga futte imasu kara, takushii de kaerimashō ka. 4. Dō shite nani mo tabete imasen ka. 5. Kaze ga tsuyoi kara, ki o tsukete kudasai.

7. 1. gi 2. a 3. i 4. ko 5. ku 6. ka 7. e 8. go 9. u 10. ki 11. ga 12. gu 13. ke 14. o 15. ge

8. 1. kēki (cake) 2. kokoa (cocoa) 3. kōku (coke) 4. ōkē (okay) 5. kāki (khaki)

Unit 12

1. 1. d 2. g 3. h 4. f 5. c 6. e 7. a 8. b

2. 1. c 2. b 3. b 4. a 5. c 6. a

3. 1. tonari 2. wakarimashita 3. amari 4. arigatō 5. futari 6. hidari 7. magarimasu 8. narimasu

4. 1. nonde 2. tabemasu 3. itte 4. narimasu 5. kaimasu 6. atte 7. hanashimasu 8. kiite 9. yonde 10. machimasu

5. 1. Massugu itte kudasai. 2. Futatsu-me no kado o migi ni magatte kudasai. 3. Hidari ni magatte kudasai. 4. (Kono) kusuri o nonde kudasai. 5. (Kono) botan o oshite kudasai. 6. Mado o shimete kudasai.

6. Across: 5. atarashii 7. ni 8. dō 9. aki 10. maiban 12. migi 13. massugu 14. niwa 16. itte 17. made 18. nonde 19. de Down: 1. kayōbi 2. wakarimasen 3. shumi 4. minna 6. arimasu 10. no 12. minami 15. dete 16. iie

7. 1. chairo, orenji, midori 2. imōto, haha, shujin 3. takushii, kuruma, ōtobai 4. doko, dore, dare 5. minami, higashi 6. furui, atarashii, mazui

8. 1. Katō san wa kaimono o shimashita ga, Satō san wa shimasen deshita. 2. Katō san mo Satō san mo Yokohama e/ni ikimashita. 3. Katō san mo Satō san mo kinō no yoru dekakemasen deshita. 4. Katō san wa Eigo o benkyō shimashita ga, Satō san wa shimasen deshita. 5. Katō san mo Satō san mo Supein ryōri no resutoran de tabemashita. 6. Katō san wa mainichi shinbun o yomimashita ga, Satō san wa yomimasen deshita.

9. 1. It was raining. 2. Some cakes. 3. Not tasty at all. 4. English study. 5. Tried to call some friends.

Unit 13

1. 1. d 2. a 3. g 4. c 5. b 6. h 7. f 8. e

2. 1. F 2. T 3. F 4. T 5. T 6. T

3. 1. atama 2. kami no ke 3. me 4. mimi 5. hana 6. kuchi 7. ha 8. kubi

4. 1. Makiko san wa, Sūzan san yori kami no ke ga nagai desu. 2. Sūzan san wa, Makiko san yori toshi o totte imasu. 3. Makiko san wa, Sūzan san yori yasete imasu. 4. Sūzan san wa, Makiko san yori yoku benkyō shimasu. 5. Makiko san wa, Sūzan san yori bōifurendo ga ōi desu. 6. Sūzan san wa, Makiko san yori, supōtsu ga jōzu desu.

5. 1. Aoi me to chairo no me to dochira no hō ga suki desu ka. Chairo no/Aoi me no hō ga suki desu. 2. Tōkyō to Kyōto to dochira no hō ga furui desu ka. Kyōto no hō ga furui desu. 3. Aki to fuyu to dochira no hō ga ame ga ōi desu ka.

Aki/Fuyu no hō ga ame ga ōi desu. 4. Terebi to bideo to dochira no hō o yoku mimasu ka. Terebi/Bideo no hō o yoku mimasu. 5. Sakana to niku to dochira no hō o yoku tabemasu ka. Sakana/Niku no hō o yoku tabemasu.

6. 1. Kātā san wa, kami no ke ga kurokute, me ga aoi desu.
2. Kubota san wa, se ga takakute, yasete imasu. 3. Yamaguchi san wa, kami no ke ga usukute, megane o kakete imasu.
4. Honda san wa, me ga ōkikute, futotte imasu. 5. Rojāzu san wa, wakakute, kami no ke ga mijikai desu.

7. 1. se 2. za 3. zo 4. shi 5. ji 6. zu 7. sa 8. su 9. so 10. ze

8. 1. b (Chicago) 2. d (whiskey) 3. a (circus) 4. b (sausage)
5. c (course)

Unit 14

1. 1. c 2. d 3. e 4. f 5. g 6. a 7. b

2. dekimasu, dekimasu, arimasu, wakarimasen, imasu, arimasu, imasen, ikimasu, ja arimasen, ikimasu, imasu

3. 1. shinkansen 2. katamichi 3. kakaru 4. seki 5. shiteiseki 6. sen 7. shuppatsu 8. guchi 9. mai 10. otona 11. konde [KIREI NA HITO]

4. 1. b 2. a 3. a 4. c 5. b

5. 1. Hiragana o yomu koto ga dekimasu/dekimasen. 2. Asa hayaku okiru koto ga dekimasu/dekimasen. 3. Furansugo (o hanasu koto) ga dekimasu/dekimasen. 4. Sashimi o taberu koto ga dekimasu/dekimasen. 5. Kēki o tsukuru koto ga dekimasu/dekimasen. 6. Oyogu koto (OR suiei) ga dekimasu/dekimasen. 7. Jōzu ni utau koto ga dekimasu/dekimasen.

6. 1. Hikōki ga kowai kara, itsumo densha ka kuruma de ryokō shimasu. 2. Itō san mo watashitachi to issho ni kuru kara, kippu o san-mai katte kudasai. 3. Kanji o yomu koto wa dekiru kedo, kaku koto wa dekimasen. 4. Densha wa 8:30 ni shuppatsu suru kara, 8:15 made ni eki e kite kudasai. 5. Mainichi benkyō suru kedo, zenzen jōzu ni narimasen. 6. Kyō wa ame ga futte iru kara, basu wa osoi desu.

7. 1. Totemo takai kaban o motte iru to omotte imasu. 2. Kekkon shite inai to omotte imasu. 3. Tōkyō ni sunde iru to omotte imasu. 4. Eigo ga sukoshi dekiru to omotte imasu. 5. Takai sūtsu o kite iru to omotte imasu.

8. 1. chi 2. da 3. do 4. te 5. zu 6. ji 7. ta 8. tsu 9. de 10. to

9. 1. gitā 2. sētā 3. tesuto 4. Doitsu 5. chiizu 6. tōsuto 7. sūtsu 8. takushii 9. dezāto 10. sōda

Unit 15

1. 1. f 2. e 3. d 4. b 5. a 6. g 7. c

2. 4-2-6-1-3-5

3. 3rd. mikka 4th. yokka 5th. itsuka 6th. muika 8th. yōka 9th. kokonoka 11th. jū-ichi-nichi 12th. jū-ni-nichi 14th. jū-yokka 15th. jū-go-nichi 16th. jū-roku-nichi 17th. jū-shichi-nichi 18th. jū-hachi-nichi 20th. hatsuka

4. 1. konsāto: concert 2. hakubutsukan: museum 3. jinja: shrine 4. bijutsukan: art gallery 5. onsen: hot springs 6. o-tera: temple 7. gekijō: theatre 8. doraibu: a drive

5. 1. Zannen desu ga, yokka no asa wa Nihongo no tesuto ga aru n' desu. 2. Zannen desu ga, suiyōbi no gogo wa, Yokohama ni iku n' desu. 3. Zannen desu ga, mokuyōbi wa haha no tanjōbi desu. 4. Zannen desu ga, nanoka wa arubeito ga aru n' desu. 5. Zannen desu ga, yōka mo kokonoka mo Nihon Arupusu ni haikingu ni iku n' desu.

6. A-B-A-A-B

7. na-2 ni-4 nu-8 ne-7 no-6

8. 1. f kanada 2. g kanū 3. i tenisu 4. a nūdo 5. c nekutai 6. j nega 7. h nōto 8. b naita 9. d nūga 10. e kajino

Unit 16

1. 1. c 2. e 3. g 4. f 5. a 6. d 7. b

2. 1. T 2. NM 3. T 4. F 5. NM 6. F

3. 1. ude (arm) 2. ashi (leg) 3. te (hand) 4. kata (shoulder) 5. hiza (knee) 6. yubi (finger) 7. o-naka (stomach) 8. koshi (waist/hips) 9. tekubi (wrist)

4. 1. sabishii 2. tsukareta 3. nodo ga kawaita 4. onaka ga suita 5. ha ga itai 6. hazukashii 7. samui 8. me ga itai

5. 1. Megane o kaketa hō ga ii desu yo. 2. Sono sētā o kita hō ga ii desu yo. 3. Hayaku kaetta hō ga ii desu yo. 4. Tabako o yameta hō ga ii desu yo. 5. Kusuri o nonda hō ga ii desu yo.

6. 1. Sūzan san mo Ikeda san mo Furansugo o benkyō shitai desu. 2. Sūzan san wa Afurika e ikitai kedo, Ikeda san wa ikitaku arimasen. 3. Sūzan san mo Ikeda san mo ōkii kuruma o kaitaku arimasen. 4. Sūzan san mo Ikeda san mo maiasa osoku okitai desu. 5. Sūzan san wa takai hoteru ni tomaritai kedo, Ikeda san wa tomaritaku arimasen.

7. (clockwise from top) po, bi, ha, be, ho, pa, he, ba, fu, pe, pi, bu, hi

8. 1. c 2. a 3. d 4. b 5. c 6. a

Unit 17

1. 1. d 2. f 3. a 4. g 5. c 6. h 7. b 8. e

2. 6-8-3-7-2-4-1-5

3. 1. dokoka 2. nanimo 3. daremo 4. dareka 5. nanika 6. daremo 7. nanimo 8. dokoka

4. 1. sawaranaide 2. toranaide 3. suwanaide 4. hairanaide 5. suwaranaide 6. tsukenaide

5. 1. Nanoka no gogo, Kawasaki de Hirota san ni Eigo o oshieru yotei desu. 2. Yōka no asa, haisha ni iku yotei desu. 3. Kokonoka no asa, haikingu kurabu no kaigi ni deru yotei desu. 4. Kokonoka no yoru, Makiko san to Furansu no eiga o mi ni iku yotei desu. 5. Tōka no yoru, Yokohama ni itte, Makiko san no uchi ni tomaru yotei desu. 6. Jū-ichi-nichi no gogo, Ginza ni itte, atarashii kutsu to doresu/wanpiisu o kau yotei desu.

6. 1. Ongaku o kiite mo ii desu. 2. Tabako o sutte mo ii desu. 3. Petto o katte wa ikemasen. 4. Pātii o shite wa ikemasen. 5. O-sake o nonde mo ii desu. 6. Yoru osoku kaette wa ikemasen.

7. 1. Ashita kaimono ni iku tsumori desu ka. Hai, iku tsumori desu./Iie, iku tsumori wa arimasen. 2. Rainen no natsu yasumi ni doko ka ni iku tsumori desu ka. (place) ni iku tsumori desu. 3. Ashita no asa osoku made nete mo ii desu

ka. Hai, ii desu./Iie, osoku made nete wa ikemasen.
4. Konshū dareka ni tegami o kakimashita ka. Hai, (person) ni tegami o kakimashita/Iie, dare ni mo tegami o kakimasen deshita. 5. Ashita no yotei wa nan desu ka. (Free answer)
6. Itsuka haisha ni iku yotei ga arimasu ka. Hai, arimasu./Iie, arimasen.

8. 1. d 2. g 3. a 4. f 5. h 6. c 7. b 8. e

9. 1. movie 2. tire 3. pessimist 4. Mexico 5. harmony 6. smart 7. yoga 8. humor

Unit 18

1. 1. e 2. g 3. f 4. b 5. c 6. h 7. a 8. d

2. 1. wa 2. ni 3. no 4. to 5. ni 6. no 7. wa 8. ga 9. ga 10. ni 11. ni 12. ga 13. no 14. wa 15. no 16. wa 17. ga

3. 1. h 2. g 3. f 4. a 5. d 6. j 7. i 8. b

4. 1. taka-sō 2. omoshiro-sō 3. takakatta 4. ureshi-sō 5. atarashii 6. oishi-sō

5. 1. Fuji san ni nobotta koto ga arimasu ka. 2. Tako o tabeta koto ga arimasu ka. 3. Kyōto e/ni itta koto ga arimasu ka. 4. Sumō o mita koto ga arimasu ka. 5. O-sake o nonda koto ga arimasu ka. 6. Kimono o kita koto ga arimasu ka.

6. 1. Nihon no karē to Indo no karē to Tai no karē no naka de, dore ga ichiban karai desu ka. (___) ga ichiban karai to omoimasu. 2. Kyōto to Ōsaka to Nagoya no naka de, doko ga Tōkyō kara ichiban tōi desu ka. Ōsaka ga ichiban tōi to omoimasu. 3. Niku to sakana to yasai no naka de, dore ga ichiban karada ni ii desu ka. (___) ga ichiban karada ni ii to omoimasu. 4. O-sake to uisukii to biiru no naka de, dore ga ichiban tsuyoi desu ka. Uisukii ga ichiban tsuyoi to omoimasu. 5. Furansu ryōri to Nihon ryōri to Chūka ryōri no naka de, dore ga ichiban takai desu ka. (___) ga ichiban takai to omoimasu. 6. Tako to ika to sashimi no naka de, dore ga ichiban suki desu ka. (___) ga ichiban suki da to omoimasu.

7. 1. c 2. f 3. d 4. a 5. h 6. g 7. b 8. e

8. 1. wine 2. celery 3. cauliflower 4. orange 5. grapefruit 6. macaroni 7. salad 8. (Japanese) curry and rice 9. ice cream 10. bacon

Unit 19

1. 1. c 2. e 3. g 4. h 5. a 6. d 7. b 8. f

2. irasshai, shimasu, tsukareta, yukkuri, okimasu, kedo, shimete, dō, go-shujin, kaeru

3. 1. e 2. a 4. d 5. f 6. c 7. b

4. 1. handoru, mawashitara 2. suitchi, oshitara 3. rebā, hiitara 4. kagi, mawashitara 5. botan, oshitara

5. 1. Gasu-dai o harau tame ni ginkō e ikimasu. 2. Imōtosan no tanjōbi no purezento o kau tame ni, Matsudō Depāto e ikimasu. 3. Raishū no kaigi no koto o sōdan suru tame ni, Honda san ni denwa shimasu. 4. Oyogu tame ni, Supōtsu Sentā e ikimasu. 5. Keiko san ni au tame ni, "Poppy" to iu kissaten e ikimasu. 6. Yoyaku o suru tame ni, haisha ni denwa shimasu.

6. 1. Iie, biiru o takusan nonde mo, futorimasen yo. 2. Iie, sūtsu wa takakute mo, kaimasu yo. 3. Iie, nagai aida oyoide mo, tsukaremasen yo. 4. Iie, Keiko san ga konakute mo, tanoshii

desu yo. 5. Iie, Honda san to sōdan shite mo, wakarimasen yo. 6. Iie, takushii de itte mo, densha ni maniaimasen yo.

7. 1. chēn sutoa (chain store) 2. byūtii saron (beauty salon) 3. jūsu (juice) 4. kyabarē (cabaret) 5. Nyū Yōku (New York) 6. festibaru (festival) 7. intabyū (interview) 8. fōkasu (focus) 9. jānarisuto (journalist) 10. matiini (martini)

8. 1. uokka-vodka 2. Yōroppa-Europe 3. sukotchi-Scotch 4. sakka-soccer 5. massāji-massage 6. messēji-message 7. raketto-racket 8. poketto-pocket 9. futtobōru-football 10. kurashikku-classic/classical

Unit 20

1. 1. e 2. g 3. h 4. f 5. b 6. a 7. c 8. d

2. 1. T 2. T 3. T 4. F 5. T 6. T

3. 1. yomeba 2. nakereba 3. nomeba 4. areba 5. wakaranakereba 6. konakereba 7. shinakereba 8. atsukereba 9. yokereba 10. nenakereba YAMA NO NAKA

4. 1. Maiasa 8:30 made ni kyōshitsu ni ikanakereba narimasen. 2. Maiasa asagohan o taberu mae ni, joggingu o shinakereba narimasen. 3. Yoru 11:30 made ni denki o kesanakereba narimasen. 4. Kenkyū sentā no naka de, kutsu o haite wa ikemasen. 5. Heya no naka de, tabete wa ikemasen. 6. Heya no naka de, sake o nonde wa ikemasen.

5. Shichi-ji ni okimasu. Okite kara, joggingu ni ikimasu. Joggingu ni itte kara, shāwā o abimasu. Shāwā o abite kara, asagohan o tabemasu. Asagohan o tabete kara, kurasu ga hajimarimasu. Yo-ji ni kurasu ga owarimasu. Kurasu ga owatte kara, supōtsu o shimasu. Supōtsu o shite kara, o-furo ni hairimasu. O-furo ni haitte kara, bangohan o tabemasu. Bangohan o tabete kara, terebi o mimasu. Terebi o mite kara, nemasu.

6. 1. b (Poland) 2. d (table) 3. a (engineer) 4. d (omelette) 5. c (nightwear)

7. 1. b (Europe) 2. d (musicals) 3. c (gin and tonic) 4. a (button) 5. c (training)

Unit 21

1. 1. c 2. e 3. f 4. a 5. d 6. b

2. 1. ga 2. wa 3. wa 4. ga 5. o 6. o 7. wa 8. ga 9. wa 10. ni 11. no 12. wa 13. o 14. o 15. o 16. no 17. wa

3. 1. futtari, yandari 2. attari, awanakattari 3. kumottari, haretari 4. tsukattari, tsukawanakattari 5. kitari, konakattari

4. 1. Biiru o nondari, uta o utattari shimashita. 2. Haretari, kumottari shimashita. 3. Kasetto o kiitari, kanji o kaitari sureba ii desu. 4. Eigo de hanashitari, Nihongo de hanashitari shimasu. 5. Yoku naitari, warattari shimashita.

5. 1. jōzu ni 2. nemui 3. kantan ni 4. hayaku 5. sabishiku

6. 1. Sūtsukēsu o kai ni itta toki, Tanaka sensei ni aimashita. 2. Tanaka sensei to hanashi o shite ita toki, ame ga furihajimemashita. 3. Kissaten ni haitta toki, totemo konde imashita. 4. Kissaten o deta toki, kasa o wasuremashita. 5. Kaeri no densha ni notta toki, atama ga itaku narimashita. 6. Uchi e kaetta toki, taihen tsukaremashita.

7. 1. 3 2. 10 3. 8 4. 6 5. 1 6. 9 7. 4 8. 2 9. 7 10. 5

8. 1. 6F, two small towels 2. 4F, nothing 3. 5F, six cheap ballpoint pens 4. 8F, had coffee in coffee shop at 2:00 5. 2F, red suitcase 6. B1, four films for camera

Unit 22

1. 1. d 2. c 3. a 4. e 5. b

2. o-hisashiburi, o-genki, moratta, ageru, haitta, o-mimai, taishita, jitsu wa, nenagara

3. 1. o-shōgatsu 2. tanjōbi 3. kekkonshiki 4. kurisumasu 5. barentain dē 6. sotsugyō 7. o-chūgen 8. o-seibo 9. bōnenkai 10. mimai

4. 1. agemashō 2. sashiagemashō 3. moraimashita 4. itadakimashita 5. yatte

5. 1. Benkyō o shinagara, terebi o miru no wa dame desu. 2. Shokuji o shinagara, shimbun o yomu no wa dame desu. 3. Denwa de hanashinagara, taberu no wa dame desu. 4. Konpyūtā o tsukainagara, kōhii o nomu no wa dame desu. 5. Beddo de nenagara, taberu no wa dame desu. 6. Shukudai o shinagara, "Walkman" o kiku no wa dame desu.

6. Dialogue 1: A1-B2-A2-B1-A2-B1
   Dialogue 2: A2-B1-A1-B2-A1-B2

7. 1. c 2. f 3. a 4. h 5. g 6. b 7. e 8. d

8. 1. scarf, birthday, Hayashi san 2. chocolate, Valentine's Day, Morita san, 3. clock, wedding, Dr (OR Professor) Yamaguchi 4. sweater, Christmas, mother

Unit 23

1. 1. d 2. g 3. e 4. h 5. a 6. b 7. c 8. f

2. 7-3-5-4-2-6-8-1

3. 1. taiya 2. kyūkō 3. kotoba 4. kawaii 5. iimasu

4. 1. kuremashita 2. agemashita 3. sashiagemashita 4. kudasaimashita 5. kuremashita 6. agemashita

5. 1. Rainen no natsu ni Ōsutoraria ni ikō to omotte imasu. 2. Kami no ke o mijikaku kitte moraō to omotte imasu. 3. Supeingo o benkyō shiyō to omotte imasu. 4. Chokorēto o yameyō to omotte imasu. 5. Atarashii kuruma o kaō to omotte imasu.

6. 1. Kono ji o yomu koto ga dekinai kara oshiete kudasai. 2. Honda san wa atarashii apāto o sagasō to omotte imasu. 3. Ima no shigoto wa suki ja nai kara yameyō to kangaete imasu.

7. 1. a 2. a 3. a 4. b 5. b

8. 1. a 2. c 3. e 4. f 5. g 6. d 7. b

9. 1. Hayashi san wa Morita san ni nani o agemashita ka. 2. Murata san to Yamada san wa kekkon suru to kikimashita ga. Hontō? 3. Tanaka san mo Kimura san mo pātii ni kite kuremashita. 4. Sumimasen ga, kore o Mori san to Yamanaka san ni okutte kudasai.

Unit 24

1. 1. e 2. f 3. g 4. a 5. d 6. b 7. h 8. c

2. 1. Itadakimasu. 2. Arigatō. 3. (O)-Hisashiburi (desu) ne. 4. Moshi moshi? 5. Irasshaimase. 6. Itte kimasu. 7. Dō itashimashite. 8. Omedetō gozaimasu.

3. Across: 1. nemui 6. mainen 8. mikka 9. utatta 12. yuki 15. atta 16. kibishii 17. seki 18. mimi 19. eki 20. kitara 23. semai 25. aite 26. ōi 27. furu
   Down: 1. nomanakereba 2. mokuyōbi 3. ima 4. niku 5. deta 7. itadakimasu 10. to 11. tatte 13. keshite 14. mijikai 21. ii 22. aru 23. se 24. mō

4. 1. a 2. c 3. b 4. b 5. a

5. 1. me, holding present 2. Mr Wada 3. father 4. Jun 5. mother, wearing glasses, 6. grandmother, holding flowers 7. Tomoko, wearing a strange hat

6. Free answers

7. 1. e 2. d 3. b 4. a 5. c

Grammar

1. HIRAGANA AND KATAKANA SYLLABARIES:

Hiragana					Katakana				
あ a	い i	う u	え e	お o	ア a	イ i	ウ u	エ e	オ o
か ka	き ki	く ku	け ke	こ ko	カ ka	キ ki	ク ku	ケ ke	コ ko
さ sa	し shi	す su	せ se	そ so	サ sa	シ shi	ス su	セ se	ソ so
た ta	ち chi	つ tsu	て te	と to	タ ta	チ chi	ツ tsu	テ te	ト to
な na	に ni	ぬ nu	ね ne	の no	ナ na	ニ ni	ヌ nu	ネ ne	ノ no
は ha	ひ hi	ふ fu	へ he	ほ ho	ハ ha	ヒ hi	フ fu	ヘ he	ホ ho
ま ma	み mi	む mu	め me	も mo	マ ma	ミ mi	ム mu	メ me	モ mo
や ya		ゆ yu		よ yo	ヤ ya		ユ yu		ヨ yo
ら ra	り ri	る ru	れ re	ろ ro	ラ ra	リ ri	ル ru	レ re	ロ ro
わ wa				を o	ワ wa				ヲ o
ん n					ン n				

2. VERBS:

This is a list of all the verbs which appear in the *Japanese Workbook,* showing the **-masu** form, the **-nai** form, and the **-te** form.

DICTIONARY FORM	-MASU FORM	-NAI FORM	-TE FORM	MEANING
abiru	abimasu	abanai	abite	pour water/shower
ageru	agemasu	agenai	agete	give
akeru	akemasu	akenai	akete	open
arau	araimasu	arawanai	aratte	wash
aru	arimasu	nai	atte	be, exist, have
aruku	arukimasu	arukanai	aruite	walk
au	aimasu	awanai	atte	meet
chigau	chigaimasu	chigawanai	chigatte	differ, be mistaken
dasu	dashimasu	dasanai	dashite	put out, send
dekakeru	dekakemasu	dekakenai	dekakete	go out
dekiru	dekimasu	dekinai	dekite	can, be able to
deru	demasu	denai	dete	go out, appear
fuku	fukimasu	fukanai	fuite	blow
furu	furimasu	furanai	futte	fall, drop
futoru	futorimasu	futoranai	futotte	become fat
ganbaru	ganbarimasu	ganbaranai	ganbatte	try hard/do one's best
hairu	hairimasu	hairanai	haitte	go in, enter
hajimaru	hajimarimasu	hajimaranai	hajimatte	begin (intrans.)
hajimeru	hajimemasu	hajimenai	hajimete	begin (trans.)
hanasu	hanashimasu	hanasanai	hanashite	speak, talk
harau	haraimasu	harawanai	haratte	pay
hareru	haremasu	harenai	harete	become clear (weather)
hiku	hikimasu	hikanai	hiite	pull
iku	ikimasu	ikanai	itte	go
ireru	iremasu	irenai	irete	put in, insert
iru	imasu	inai	ite	be, exist
itadaku	itadakimasu	itadakanai	itadaite	receive
iu	iimasu	iwanai	itte	say, relate
kaburu	kaburimasu	kaburanai	kabutte	wear (on the head)
kaeru	kaerimasu	kaeranai	kaette	return/go home
kakaru	kakarimasu	kakaranai	kakatte	take (time), last
kakeru	kakemasu	kakenai	kakete	call, phone
kaku	kakimasu	kakanai	kaite	write
kangaeru	kangaemasu	kangaenai	kangaete	think about
kasu	kashimasu	kasanai	kashite	lend
kau	kaimasu	kawanai	katte	buy
kawaku	kawakimasu	kawakanai	kawatte	become dry
kesu	keshimasu	kesanai	keshite	turn off
kieru	kiemasu	kienai	kiete	go out, die out
kiku	kikimasu	kikanai	kiite	hear, ask
kiru	kirimasu	kiranai	kitte	cut
kiru	kimasu	kinai	kite	wear
komu	komimasu	komanai	konde	be crowded
kotaeru	kotaemasu	kotaenai	kotaete	answer, reply
kudasaru	kudasaimasu	kudasaranai	kudasatte	give
kumoru	kumorimasu	kumoranai	kumotte	be cloudy
kureru	kuremasu	kurenai	kurete	give

DICTIONARY FORM	-MASU FORM	-NAI FORM	-TE FORM	MEANING
kuru	kimasu	konai	kite	come
magaru	magarimasu	magaranai	magatte	turn
maniau	maniaimasu	maniawanai	maniatte	be in time
matsu	machimasu	matanai	matte	wait
mawasu	mawashimasu	mawasanai	mawatte	turn
migaku	migakimasu	migakanai	migaite	brush
miru	mimasu	minai	mite	see, watch
morau	moraimasu	morawanai	moratte	receive
motsu	mochimasu	motanai	motte	hold, have
naku	nakimasu	nakanai	naite	cry
nakunaru	nakunarimasu	nakunaranai	nakunatte	be lost, die
narabu	narabimasu	narabanai	narande	line up, queue
naosu	naoshimasu	naosanai	naoshite	mend
narau	naraimasu	narawanai	naratte	learn
naru	narimasu	naranai	natte	become, get
neru	nemasu	nenai	nete	sleep, go to bed
noboru	noborimasu	noboranai	nobotte	climb, go up
nomu	nomimasu	nomanai	nonde	drink
noru	norimasu	noranai	notte	get in/on, ride
nugu	nugimasu	nuganai	nuide	take off
oboeru	oboemasu	oboenai	oboete	remember, recall
okiru	okimasu	okinai	okite	get up
okoru	okorimasu	okoranai	okotte	get angry
oku	okimasu	okanai	oite	put, place
okuru	okurimasu	okuranai	okutte	send
omou	omoimasu	omowanai	omotte	think
oshieru	oshiemasu	oshienai	oshiete	teach, tell
osu	oshimasu	osanai	oshite	push
owaru	owarimasu	owaranai	owatte	end, finish
sagasu	sagashimasu	sagasanai	sagashite	look for
sashiageru	sashiagemasu	sashiagenai	sashiagete	give
sawaru	sawarimasu	sawaranai	sawatte	touch
shimeru	shimemasu	shimenai	shimete	close
suku	sukimasu	sukanai	suite	become empty
sumu	sumimasu	sumanai	sunde	live, reside
suru	shimasu	shinai	shite	do
suu	suimasu	suwanai	sutte	smoke
suwaru	suwarimasu	suwaranai	suwatte	sit down
taberu	tabemasu	tabenai	tabete	eat
tatsu	tachimasu	tatanai	tatte	stand up
tetsudau	tetsudaimasu	tetsudawanai	tetsudatte	help
todokeru	todokemasu	todokenai	todokete	deliver
tomaru	tomarimasu	tomaranai	tomatte	stay over
tomeru	tomemasu	tomenai	tomete	stop, halt
toru	torimasu	toranai	totte	take
tsukareru	tsukaremasu	tsukarenai	tsukarete	become tired
tsukau	tsukaimasu	tsukawanai	tsukatte	use
tsuku	tsukimasu	tsukanai	tsuite	arrive
tsukuru	tsukurimasu	tsukuranai	tsukutte	make
ukeru	ukemasu	ukenai	ukete	get, receive
umareru	umaremasu	umarenai	umarete	be born
utau	utaimasu	utawanai	utatte	sing

DICTIONARY FORM	-MASU FORM	-NAI FORM	-TE FORM	MEANING
wakaru	wakarimasu	wakaranai	wakatte	understand
warau	waraimasu	warawanai	waratte	laugh
wasureru	wasuremasu	wasurenai	wasurete	forget
yameru	yamemasu	yamenai	yamete	quit, stop
yamu	yamimasu	yamanai	yande	stop, be over
yaru	yarimasu	yaranai	yatte	give
yaseru	yasemasu	yasenai	yasete	become slim
yomu	yomimasu	yomanai	yonde	read

3. DAYS OF THE WEEK:

Monday	getsuyōbi
Tuesday	kayōbi
Wednesday	suiyōbi
Thursday	mokuyōbi
Friday	kinyōbi
Saturday	doyōbi
Sunday	nichiyōbi

4. DATES:

1st tsuitachi	11th jū-ichi-nichi	21st ni-jū-ichi-nichi
2nd futsuka	12th jū-ni-nichi	22nd ni-jū-ni-nichi
3rd mikka	13th jū-san-nichi	23rd ni-jū-san-nichi
4th yokka	14th jū-yokka	24th ni-jū-yokka
5th itsuka	15th jū-go-nichi	25th ni-jū-go-nichi
6th muika	16th jū-roku-nichi	26th ni-jū-roku-nichi
7th nanoka	17th jū-shichi-nichi	27th ni-jū-shichi-nichi
8th yōka	18th jū-hachi-nichi	28th ni-jū-hachi-nichi
9th kokonoka	19th jū-ku-nichi	29th ni-jū-ku-nichi
10th tōka	20th hatsuka	30th san-jū-nichi
		31st san-jū-ichi-nichi

Examples:

Haha no tanjōbi wa san-gatsu jū-go-nichi desu. (My mother's birthday is March 15th.)

Hachi-gatsu tōka kara ku-gatsu futsuka made imashita. (We were there from August 10th to September 2nd.)

5. ADJECTIVES:

POSITIVE	NEGATIVE	PAST POSITIVE	PAST NEGATIVE
-i adjectives:			
atsui	atsuku arimasen	atsukatta	atsuku arimasen deshita
(hot)	(not hot)	(was hot)	(wasn't hot)
chiisai	chiisaku arimasen	chiisakatta	chiisaku arimasen deshita
(small)	(not small)	(was small)	(wasn't small)

POSITIVE	NEGATIVE	PAST POSITIVE	PAST NEGATIVE
ii	yoku arimasen	yokatta	yoku arimasen deshita
(good)	(not good)	(was good)	(wasn't good)
-na adjectives			
jōzu desu	jōzu ja arimasen	jōzu deshita	jōzu ja arimasen deshita
(good at)	(not good at)	(was good at)	(wasn't good at)
iya	iya ja arimasen	iya deshita	iya ja arimasen deshita
(horrible)	(not horrible)	(was horrible)	(wasn't horrible)

Examples:

Kotoshi no shichi-gatsu wa taihen atsukatta desu ga, hachi-gatsu wa zenzen atsuku arimasen deshita. (July was really hot this year, but August wasn't hot at all.)

Tenisu ga suki da kedo, amari jōzu ja arimasen. (I like tennis, but I'm not very good at it.)

6. NUMBERS:

1	ichi	20	ni-jū	500	go-hyaku	8,000	has-sen
2	ni	30	san-jū	600	rop-pyaku	9,000	kyū-sen
3	san	40	yon/shi-jū	700	nana-hyaku	10,000	ichi-man
4	shi/yon	50	go-jū	800	hap-pyaku	30,000	san-man
5	go	60	roku-jū	900	kyū-hyaku	100,000	jū-man
6	roku	70	nana/shichi-jū	1,000	sen	500,000	go-jū-man
7	shichi/nana	80	hachi-jū	2,000	ni-sen	800,000	hachi-jū-man
8	hachi	90	kyū/ku-jū	3,000	san-zen	1,000,000	hyaku-man
9	kyū/ku	100	hyaku	4,000	yon-sen	5,000,000	go-hyaku-man
10	jū	200	ni-hyaku	5,000	go-sen	10,000,000	is-sen-man
11	jū-ichi	300	san-byaku	6,000	roku-sen		
12	jū-ni	400	yon-hyaku	7,000	nana-sen		

Examples:

Ikura? Go-man nana-sen go-hyaku en? Chotto takai desu ne! (How much is it? ¥57,500? That's a bit expensive, isn't it!)

Tōkyō kara Rondon made wa kyū-sen go-hyaku roku-jū kiro desu. (It's 9,560 kilometers from Tokyo to London.)

7. Counters:

	PEOPLE	LONG, THIN THINGS	MINUTES	THIN, FLAT THINGS
1	hitori	ip-pon	ip-pun	ichi-mai
2	futari	ni-hon	ni-fun	ni-mai
3	san-nin	san-bon	san-pun	san-mai
4	yo-nin	yon-hon	yon-pun	yon-mai
5	go-nin	go-hon	go-fun	go-mai
6	roku-nin	rop-pon	rop-pun	roku-mai
7	shichi-nin	nana-hon	nana-fun	shichi-mai
8	hachi-nin	hap-pon	hap-pun/hachi-fun	hachi-mai
9	kyū-nin	kyū-hon	kyū-fun	kyū-mai
10	jū-nin	jū-hon	jup-pun/jip-pun	jū-mai
11	jū-ichi-nin	jū-ip-pon	jū-ip-pun	jū-ichi-mai
how many?	nan-nin	nan-bon	nan-pun	nan-mai

COUNTING OBJECTS:

1	hitotsu	6	muttsu
2	futatsu	7	nanatsu
3	mittsu	8	yattsu
4	yottsu	9	kokonotsu
5	itsutsu	10	tō
		how many?	ikutsu

Examples:

Kōhii o mittsu kudasai. (Three coffees, please.)

Biiru nan-bon nomimashita ka. (How many bottles of beer did you drink?)

Mō san-jip-pun matte imasu. (I've already been waiting 30 minutes.)

Tomodachi san-nin to issho ni yama e ikimashita. (I went to the mountains with three friends.)

100-en kitte o san-mai kudasai. (Three ¥100 stamps, please.)

8. KO-, SO-, A-, DO- WORDS

koko	soko	asoko	doko
here	there	over there	where?
kore	sore	are	dore
this one	that one	that one over there	which one?
kono	sono	ano	dono
this [adj]	that	that … over there	which?
konna	sonna	anna	donna
this kind of	that kind of	that kind of … over there	what kind of?
kochira	sochira	achira	dochira
this way	that way	that way over there	which way?

Glossary

After each entry in the Glossary you'll find the number of the unit in which the word first occurs.

A

abiru/abimasu	pour (water) over oneself (=have a shower) 20
abunai	dangerous 13
ageru/agemasu	give 22
aida	between 4
aisu sukēto	ice skating 5
aite iru/imasu	be free, unoccupied 14
akai	red 7
akeru/akemasu	open 10
aki	autumn, fall 9
amai	sweet-tasting 7
amari	not very much 5
ame	rain 11
Amerika	USA 1
Amerikajin	an American 1
anata	you 14
ane	(my) older sister 6
ani	(my) older brother 6
ano	that … over there [adj.] 3
anzen-na	safe 13
aoi	blue-green 7
apāto	apartment 3
arau/araimasu	wash 20
arigatō	thank you 1
aru/arimasu	be, there is/are (inanimate), have 3
arubaito	side job, part-time job 2
aruku/arukimasu	walk 20
asa	morning 8
asagohan	breakfast 5
ashi	leg/foot 16
ashita	tomorrow 9
asoko	over there 3
atama	head 13
atarashii	new 2
atatakai	warm 9
ato de	later, after 10
atsui	hot 7
au/aimasu	meet 6

B

baiten	sales stand 14
ban	evening 9
bangō	number 1
bangohan	dinner, evening meal 5
Barentain Dē	Valentine's Day 22
basu	bus 8

beddo	bed 4
benkyō	study 9
bideo	video 2
biiru	beer 1
bijutsukan	art gallery 15
bōifurendo	boyfriend 13
boku	I, me [male] 14
bōnenkai	year-end party 22
bōringu	bowling 5
bōru	ball 4
bōshi	hat 11
botan	button 10
buchō	department head 22
burausu	blouse 3
burū	blue 7
byōin	hospital 22
byōki	ill 8

C

chairo	brown 7
chan	[familiar form of san] 3
chichi	(my) father 6
chigau/chigaimasu	that's not correct [Lit: be different] 1
chiizu	cheese 9
chiizukēki	cheesecake 7
chika ikkai	first floor basement 3
chikatetsu	subway train 8
chokorēto	chocolate 7
chotto	just a little 3
chūka ryōri	Chinese food 18

D

dai-kirai desu	dislike very much, hate 5
dai-suki desu	like very much, love 5
daidokoro	kitchen 19
daigaku	university 4
daigakusei	university student 6
daiji-na	important, serious 16
daijōbu	okay, fine 8
dakara	so, therefore 9
dake	only, just 5
dame	no good, useless 6
dare mo	no one 14
dare no	whose? 3
dare	who? 3
dareka	someone 17
daremo	no one 17

handobaggu	handbag 3
handoru	handle 19
harau/haraimasu	pay 19
hareru/haremasu	clear up (weather) 21
haru	spring 9
hashi	bridge 24
hashi	chopsticks 18
hayai	early 2
hazukashii	shy, embarrassed 16
hen-na	odd, strange 21
heta	unskillful, bad at 6
heya	room 3
hidari	left side 9
hidoi	terrible, severe 23
higashi	east 10
hikidashi	drawer 4
hikōki	plane 8
hiku/hikimasu	pull 19
hikui	low 13
hirugohan	lunch 5
hisashiburi desu	it's been a long time 22
hisho	secretary 23
hito	person 9
hitotachi	people 14
hitotsu	one (item) 10
hiza	knee 16
hō	direction, side 13
hōmu	platform 14
hon	book 1
-hon/pon	[counter for long, thin objects] 21
hoteru	hotel 17
hotto	hot coffee 4
hyaku	hundred 7

I

ichi	one 1
ichi-nichi	one day 19
ichi-nichi-jū	all day 15
ichiban	no. one, most, -est 18
ichido	once, one time 18
ie	house 24
Igirisu	England, Britain 1
Igirisujin	an English/British person 1
ii/yoi	good, fine, OK 1
iie	no 1
ika	squid 18
ikaga	how? how about? 15
ikemasen	it won't do 17
ikkai	first floor 3
iku/ikimasu	go 5
ikura	how much? 7
ima	now, at the moment 4
imi	meaning 13
imōto	(my) younger sister 6
imōtosan	(your) younger sister 6
inaka	countryside 16
Indo	India 5

inu	dog 3
ippai	full, lots of 21
irasshaimase	welcome 4
ireru/iremasu	put in, insert 10
iro	color 7
iroiro-na	various, all kinds of 9
iru/imasu	be, there is/are) 3
isha	doctor 23
isogashii	busy 15
issho ni	together 5
isu	chair 4
itadakimasu	bon appetit 18
itadaku/itadakimasu	receive 22
itai	painful, hurting 16
Itaria	Italy 1
itsu	when? 15
itsuka	fifth of the month 15
itsuka	sometime 17
itsumo	always 5
itte 'rasshai	[Lit: go and come back!] 'bye! 19
itte kimasu	[Lit: I'm going, and I'll be back!] 'bye! 19
iu/iimasu	say, speak 9
iya-na	horrible 11

J

ja arimasen	isn't, aren't 2
ja	well, well then 5
jaketto	jacket 3
jama	hindrance, interference 19
-ji	o'clock 2
jibun	one's self 22
jikan	time, hour 1
-jin	person (of country etc.) 1
jinja	temple 15
jisho	dictionary 21
jitsu wa	the truth is ... 14
jiyūseki	unreserved seat 14
joggingu	jogging 20
jōzu	skillful, good at 9
jū	ten 1
jūsho	address 10
jūsu	juice 3

K

ka	[question marker] 1
ka	or 14
kaban	bag, briefcase 1
kabuki	kabuki (Japanese theater style) 5
kaburu/kaburimasu	wear (on the head) 11
kachō	section boss 17
kado	street corner 10
kaeru/kaerimasu	return, go home 5
kagi	key 3
-kai	[counter for floors] 3
kaidan	steps, stairs 19
kaigi	meeting 8

kaimono	shopping [noun] 6	kieru/kiemasu	go out, die out 19
kaisha	company, office 5	kiiro	yellow 7
kakaru/kakarimasu	catch, start (engine) 19	kikai	machine 10
kakaru/kakarimasu	take (time) 14	kiku/kikimasu	hear, listen to 5
kakeru/kakemasu	wear (glasses) 13	kimochi	feeling 16
kaku/kakimasu	write 5	kinō	yesterday 9
kamera	camera 3	kinyōbi	Friday 8
kami/kami no ke	hair 13	kippu	ticket 14
kamo shirenai	maybe, perhaps 21	kirai desu	dislike 5
Kanada	Canada 1	kirei-na	pretty, clean 14
Kanadajin	a Canadian 1	kiru/kirimasu	cut 23
kanai	(my) wife 6	kiru/kimasu	wear 11
kanashii	sad 21	kissaten	coffee shop 2
kangaeru/kangaemasu	consider, think about 23	kita	north 12
kanji	Chinese character 14	kitanai	dirty, untidy 4
kanjō	check, bill 18	kōcha	tea 2
kanojo	she, her 5	kochira	this, here 15
kanpai	Cheers! 6	kodomo	child 9
kantan	simple, uncomplicated 7	kōhii	coffee 2
kao	face 13	koko	here 3
kara	because 8	kokonoka	ninth of the month 15
kara	from 1	komu/komimasu	be crowded 14
karai	hot, spicy 18	konban	this evening 4
karaoke bā	karaoke bar 15	kono	this [adj.] 3
kare	he, him 16	konpyūtā	computer 1
karē raisu	curry & rice (Japanese style) 18	konsāto	concert 4
karui	light (in weight) 13	koshi	waist/hips 16
kasa	umbrella 11	kotaeru/kotaemasu	answer, reply 15
kasetto tēpu	cassette tape 4	kōto	coat 3
kasu/kashimasu	lend 23	koto ga dekiru/ dekimasu	can, be able to 14
kata	shoulder 16		
katamichi	one-way ticket 14	koto	thing, fact 9
kau/kaimasu	buy 8	kotoba	word, phrase 23
kau/kaimasu	keep (animals), raise 17	kowai	frightening, fearful 13
kawaii	cute 23	kozutsumi	parcel 19
kawaisō	pity, poor 23	kubi	neck 13
kawaku/kawakimasu	become dry 16	kuchi	mouth 13
kawari ni	instead of, replacement 23	kudasai	please give me 4
kawari	second helping 18	kudasaru/kudasaimasu	give 23
kayōbi	Tuesday 8	kukkii	cookie 19
kaze	a cold 16	kūkō	airport 8
kaze o hiku/hikimasu	catch a cold 16	kumoru/kumorimasu	cloud over 21
kaze	wind 11	kurasu	class 1
kazoku	family 9	kureru/kuremasu	give 23
kedo	but, however 9	Kurisumasu	Christmas 22
keizai	economics 9	kuroi	black 7
kēki	cake 4	kuru/kimasu	come 6
kekkō	enough, very good 18	kuruma	car 1
kekkon	marriage 14	kurushii	distressing, trying 23
kekkonshiki	wedding ceremony 22	kusuri	medicine 10
kenka	argument 5	kutsu	shoes 3
kenkyū	research, study 20	kutsushita	socks 11
kenshū	study, mastery 20	kyō	today 2
kesa	this morning 9	kyōdai	brothers and sisters 9
kesu/keshimasu	turn off 20	kyōkasho	text/reference book 23
ki o tsukete kudasai	please be careful 10	kyonen	last year 9
ki	tree 11	kyōshitsu	classroom 20
kibishii	severe, strict 13	kyū/ku	nine 1

kyūkō	express train 14
kyūryō	salary 23
kyūryō-bi	pay day 23

M

mā-mā	so-so 5
mada	still, yet 6
made ni	by, not later than 20
made	until, as far as 2
mado	window 4
mae	in front of 10
magaru/magarimasu	turn 10
-mai	counter for flat objects 14
maiasa	every morning 20
maiban	every evening 6
mainen	every year 24
mainichi	every day 7
maishū	every week 24
man	ten thousand 7
maniau/maniaimasu	be in time 19
massugu	straight ahead 10
matsu/machimasu	wait 10
mawasu/mawashimasu	turn 19
mazu	first of all, at first 10
mazui	bad-tasting 7
me	eye 9
megane	glasses 7
meishi	name/business card 1
mensetsu	interview 9
mezurashii	unusual, strange 20
mi ni iku/ikimasu	go to see 15
midori	green 7
migaku/migakimasu	brush 20
migi	right (side) 10
mijikai	short 13
mikka	third of the month 15
mimai ni iku/ikimasu	go to visit (in hospital) 22
mimi	ears 13
minami	south 10
minna	everyone, all 5
miru/mimasu	see, look at 5
miruku	milk 22
mise	shop 14
mizu	water 4
mō	already, not any more 2
mō ichido	once more, again 10
mo	too, also 3
mochiron	of course 19
mōfu	blanket 19
mokuyōbi	Thursday 8
mondai	problem 4
mono	thing, object 22
morau/moraimasu	receive 22
moshi moshi	Hello? [on the phone] 6
motsu/mochimasu	hold 11
muika	sixth of the month 15
murasaki	purple 7
musuko	(my) son 8

musume	(my) daughter 22
muzukashii	difficult 7
myūjikaru	a musical 20

N

nado	and so on, et cetera 20
nagai aida	long time 22
nagai	long 13
naifu	knife 4
naka	in, inside 4
naku/nakimasu	cry 21
nakunaru/ nakunarimasu	be lost, missing, die 21
namae	name 1
nan	what? 1
nan-ban	what number? 3
nan-nin	how many people? 9
nani mo	nothing 11
nana	seven 1
nanigo	what language? 21
nanika	something 15
nankai	which floor? 3
nanoka	seventh of the month 15
naosu/naoshimasu	mend, correct 23
napukin	napkin 4
narau/naraimasu	learn 21
naru/narimasu	become 8
natsu	summer 9
ne	isn't it, aren't they, etc. 1
nekkuresu	necklace 23
neko	cat 3
nekutai	necktie 3
nemui	sleepy 18
nen	year 9
neru/nemasu	sleep, go to bed 5
netsu	temperature, fever 16
ni	in, at 3
ni	two 1
nichiyobi	Sunday 8
Nihon	Japan 1
Nihongo	Japanese language 2
niku	meat 13
nimotsu	luggage 14
-nin	[counter for people] 9
nishi	west 12
niwa	garden 3
no	[sentence ending, used by women] 16
no	of, __'s 1
noboru/noborimasu	climb 18
nodo ga kawaita	become thirsty 16
nodo	throat 16
nomimono	drinks 14
nomu/nomimasu	drink 5
noru/norimasu	get on, travel on (transportation) 18
nugu/nugimasu	take off, remove 20
nyūsu	news 6

O

o-bāsan	grandmother 24
o-cha	green tea 2
o-chūgen	mid-year gift-giving season 22
o-furo	bath 19
o-genki desu ka	How are you? 4
o-hairi kudasai	please come in 19
o-jama shimasu	excuse me for interrupting 19
o-jisan	uncle 21
o-kaeri nasai	welcome home 19
o-kage sama de	I'm fine, thank you. 4
o-kane	money 8
o-kāsan	(your) mother 6
o-kyakusan	customer, guest 4
o-naka	stomach 11
o-naka ga suita	be hungry 16
o-nēsan	(your) older sister 6
o-niisan	(your) older brother 6
o-seibo	summer gift-giving season 22
o-toire	toilet 19
o-tōsan	(your) father 6
o-tsuri	change [money] 23
oboeru/oboemasu	remember, recall 15
ōfuku	round trip ticket 14
ōi	many, lots of 13
oishii	tasty, good (taste) 7
ōkii	big 3
okiru/okimasu	get up 5
okoru/okorimasu	get angry 21
oku/okimasu	put, place 10
okuru/okurimasu	send 19
okusan	(your) wife 6
omedetō gozaimasu	congratulations 6
omoi	heavy 13
omoshiroi	interesting, entertaining 8
omou/omoimasu	think 9
onaji	same 4
onegai shimasu	please, please do that 6
ongaku	music 7
onsen	hot springs 15
opera	opera 6
orenji	orange 7
oshieru/oshiemasu	teach, tell 9
osoi	late 2
osu/oshimasu	push, press 10
ōtobai	motorcycle 3
otoko	man 24
otoko no ko	boy 24
otona	adult 14
otōto	(my) younger brother 6
ototoi	day before yesterday 9
otōtosan	(your) younger brother 6
ototoshi	year before last 9
oyogu/oyogimasu	swim 14

P

pai	pie 7
pajama	pyjamas 3
pantsu	pants, trousers 3
pan-ya	baker's 23
pātii	party 15
petto	pet 3
pinku	pink 7
purezento	present 8
pūru	swimming pool 20

R

raishū	next week 15
rajio	radio 2
rasshu	rush hour 14
rebā	lever 19
rekishi	history 20
remon	lemon 7
renshū	practice 20
repōto	report 8
resutoran	restaurant 3
rokkā	locker 3
roku	six 1
ryōkan	Japanese-style inn 18
ryokō	travel 14
ryōri	cooking, cuisine 5

S

sabishii	lonely 16
sagasu/sagashimasu	look for 23
-sai	years old 6
saifu	purse, wallet 23
sain o suru/shimasu	to sign 23
sakana	fish 13
saka-ya	sake/wine shop 23
sake	sake, rice wine 17
saki ni	ahead, before 20
sakkā	soccer 11
samui	cold 7
san	Mr, Mrs, Miss, Ms 1
san	three 1
sashiageru/ sashiagemasu	give (to person of higher status) 22
sashimi	raw fish 14
sawaru/sawarimasu	touch 17
se	height 13
sei	fault, owing to 16
seki	cough 16
seki ga deru/demasu	have a cough 16
seki	seat, place 14
semai	narrow, small (space) 19
sen	thousand 7
-sen	track number __ 14
sensei	teacher 1
senshū	last week 9
sērusu	sales 8
sētā	sweater 3
setsumei	explanation 14
shachō	company president 22
shashin	photograph 17
shatsu	shirt 3

shāwā	shower 20	suniikā	sneakers 11
shi	four 1	supagettii	spaghetti 4
shi	and also [to join sentences] 22	Supein	Spain 2
shichi/nana	seven 1	supōtsu sentā	sports center 6
shigoto	work, job 4	supōtsu uēa	sportswear 3
shii dii	CD, compact disk 4	supūn	spoon 4
shimeru/shimemasu	close 17	surippa	slippers 19
shinbun	newspaper 5	suru/shimasu	do 5
shingō	traffic signal 10	sushi	sushi, raw fish on rice 6
Shinkansen	Bullet Train 14	sutereo	stereo 3
shinnyūshain	new employees 20	sūtsu	suit 3
shinsetsu-na	kind, courteous 13	sūtsukēsu	suitcase 14
shiroi	white 7	suu/suimasu	smoke 17
shisha	branch office 8	suwaru/suwarimasu	sit down 11
shita	under, below 4	suzushii	cool 9
shiteiseki	reserved seat 14		
shitsumon	question 9	**T**	
shitsurei desu ga	excuse me, but .. 1	T-shatsu	T-shirt 11
shitsurei shimasu	excuse me 1	-ta hō ga ii desu	it's better to __ 16
shizuka-na	quiet, peaceful 3	tabako	cigarettes 17
shōgatsu	new year 22	tabe ni iku/ikimasu	go to eat 16
shokudō-sha	restaurant car 14	tabemono	food 14
shōsetsu	novel 23	taberu/tabemasu	eat 5
shōyu	soy sauce 18	tabi	journey, trip 14
shujin	(my) husband 6	tadaima	I'm back! 19
shukudai	homework 21	tada	only, just 19
shūmatsu	weekend 8	Tai	Thailand 18
shumi	interests, hobbies 9	taipu	typing 20
shuppatsu	departure 14	taishita	serious, important 22
shutchō	business trip 8	taiya	tire 4
-sō	looks like, seems 18	takai	high, expensive 7
sō desu	that's right 1	tako	octopus 18
soba	near, by 4	takusan	many, a lot of 4
sōdan suru/shimasu	discuss 19	takushii	taxi 8
sofā	sofa 4	tame ni	for the purpose of 19
soko	there 3	tanjōbi	birthday 5
sonna ni	that much/to that extent 9	tanoshii	fun, enjoyable 9
sono	that [adj.] 3	taoru	towel 19
sore kara	and also 7	tatemono	building 10
sorede	and then, so 13	tatsu/tachimasu	stand up 11
sorosoro	little by little, soon 22	te	hand 16
soto	outside 10	tēburu	table 11
sotsugyō	graduation 22	tegami	letter 6
subarashii	wonderful, marvellous 10	tekubi	wrist 16
sūgaku	mathematics 20	ten	point 21
sugoi	amazing, incredible 21	tenisu raketto	tennis racket 4
sugu	soon, immediately 5	tenki	weather 11
suiei	swimming 9	tera	temple 15
suitchi	switch 17	terebi	television 1
suiyōbi	Wednesday 8	tesuto	test 4
sukāfu	scarf 3	to	and 3
sukāto	skirt 3	todokeru/todokemasu	deliver 23
suki desu	like 5	tōi	far 18
sukii	skiing 11	tōka	tenth of the month 15
sukoshi	a little, a few 6	tokei	clock, watch 3
suku/sukimasu	become empty 16	toki	time, the time when 9
sumimasen	excuse me 1	tokidoki	sometimes 6
sumu/sumimasu	live, reside 9	tokorode	by the way 15

toko-ya	barber's 23
tomaru/tomarimasu [intransitive] 14	stay, stop, halt
tomeru/tomemasu [transitive] 10	stop, halt
tomodachi	friend 2
tonari	next to 4
torēningu	training 20
toru/torimasu	take 17
toshi	age, years 13
toshi o toru/torimasu	become old 13
toshokan	library 11
totemo	very 4
tsugi	next, following 10
tsuitachi	first of the month 15
tsukareru/tsukaremasu	become tired 16
tsukau/tsukaimasu	use 10
tsukeru/tsukemasu	light, switch on 17
tsuku/tsukimasu	arrive 24
tsuku/tsukimasu	become turned on, ignited 19
tsukue	desk 4
tsukuru/tsukurimasu	make 5
tsumaranai	boring, uninteresting 7
tsumori	intention 17
tsuyoi	strong 11

U

uchi	home, house 3
ude	arm 16
ue	on, above 4
uētoresu	waitress 24
uisukii	whiskey 6
ukeru/ukemasu	get, receive 20
umai	skillful, tasty, good 13
umareru/umaremasu	be born 9
umi	sea 11
untenshu	driver 23
ura	back, behind 11
urayamashii	envious 21
ureshii	happy 18
uriba	sales counter 14
urusai	noisy 6
ushiro	behind 4
uso	untrue, a lie 6
usui	thin, pale 13
uta	song 15
utau/utaimasu	sing 14

W

wa	[marks the topic of the sentence/phrase] 1
wain	wine 1
wakai	young 13

wakarimashita	I understand, I see 4
wakaru/wakarimasu	know, understand 5
wanpiisu	dress 11
warau/waraimasu	laugh, smile 13
warui	bad 8
wasureru/wasuremasu	forget 21
watashi	I, me 1
watashitachi	we, us 5

Y

ya	and, or 16
yakusoku	appointment, engagement 16
yakyū	baseball 15
yama	mountain 7
yameru/yamemasu	quit, stop 16
yamu/yamimasu	stop, be over 21
yaoya	grocery store, greengrocer's 23
yaru/yarimasu	give (to small child or pet) 22
yasai	vegetables 18
yasashii	easy 19
yaseru/yasemasu	become slim 13
yasete iru	be slim 13
yasui	cheap 7
yo	[sentence ending to show emphasis]
yōi	preparations 20
yōka	eighth of the month 15
yokka	fourth of the month 15
yoku	often, usually, well 6
yomu/yomimasu	read 5
yon	four 1
yonaka	middle of the night 21
yori	(more) than 13
yoru	evening, night 8
yotei	plan, appointment 17
yowai	weak 13
yoyaku	reservation 17
yubi	finger 16
yubinkyoku	post office 10
yuki	bound for (Osaka) 14
yuki	snow 11
yukkuri shite kudasai	take it easy 10
yukkuri	slowly 10

Z

zannen	pity, unfortunate 15
zasshi	magazine 4
zenbu	all, entirely 7
zenzen	not at all, never 6
zero	zero 1
zubon	pants, trousers 11
zutto	by far, much more 13